KidCoder™ Series

KidCoder™: Advanced Web Design

Student Textbook

First Edition

Copyright 2013

Homeschool Programming, Inc.

Thanks to Kathy Steffan for
helping put this course together.

KidCoder^{TM}: Advanced Web Design

Copyright © 2013 by Homeschool Programming, Inc.

980 Birmingham Rd, Suite 501-128, Alpharetta, GA 30004

ISBN: **978-0-9887033-3-9**

Contact Us

You may contact Homeschool Programming, Inc. through the information and links provided on our website: http://www.HomeschoolProgramming.com. We welcome your comments and questions regarding this course or other related programming courses you would like to study!

Other Courses

Homeschool Programming, Inc. currently has two product lines for students: the *KidCoder*^{TM} series and the *TeenCoder*^{TM} series. Our *KidCoder*^{TM} series provides easy, step-by-step programming curriculum for 4th through 12th graders. These courses use readily available software products that come shipped with the operating system or are free to install in order to teach introductory programming concepts in a fun, graphical manner. Our *TeenCoder*^{TM} series provides introductory programming curriculum for high-school students. These courses are college-preparatory material designed for the student who may wish to pursue a career in Computer Science or enhance their transcript with a technical elective.

3rd Party Copyrights

Instructional Videos

This course may be accompanied by optional Instructional Videos. These Flash-based videos will play directly from a DVD drive on the student's computer. Instructional Videos are supplements to the Student Textbook, covering every chapter and lesson with fun, animated re-enforcement of the main topics.

Instructional Videos are intended for students who enjoy a more audio-visual style of learning. They are not replacements for the Student Textbook which is still required to complete this course. However, by watching the Instructional Videos first, students may begin each textbook chapter and lesson already having some grasp of the material to be read. Where applicable, the videos will also show "screencasts" of a real programmer demonstrating some concept or activity within the software development environment.

This Student Textbook and accompanying material are all you need to complete the course successfully. Instructional Videos are optional for students who would benefit from the alternate presentation of the material. For more information or to purchase the videos separately, please refer to the product descriptions on our website: http://www.HomeschoolProgramming.com.

Table of Contents

Before You Begin

Please read the following topics before you begin the course.

Minimum Hardware and Software Requirements

This is a hands-on web design course! You will be writing HTML, reviewing supplemental course material, and working with files on your computer. Your computer must meet the following minimum requirements in order to successfully complete the assignments.

Computer Hardware

Your computer must meet the following minimum specifications:

	Minimum
CPU	1.6GHz or faster processor
RAM	1024 MB
Display	1024 x 768 video card
Hard Disk Size	3GB available space
DVD Drive	DVD-ROM drive

Operating Systems

In order to install the course software, your computer operating system must match one of the following:

Windows XP (x86) with Service Pack 3 or above
Windows Vista (x86 and x64) with Service Pack 2 or above
Windows 7 (x86 and x64)
Windows 8 (all versions except RT)
Mac OS X 10.5.8 or greater

Supported Web Browsers

You can use nearly any web browser on any computer system to view HTML. However some browsers display HTML differently. We have tested course material on current versions of the following browsers:

Internet Explorer   Mozilla Firefox   Google Chrome   Apple Safari

Conventions Used in This Text

This course will use certain styles (fonts, borders, etc.) to highlight text of special interest.

```
HTML source code will be in 11-point Consolas font, in a single box like this.
```

Property names will be in **12-point Consolas bold** text. For example: **#content{}**.

HTML elements and important terms will be in **bold face** type such as <**body**>.

This picture highlights important concepts within a lesson.

Sidebars may contain additional information, tips, or background material.

A chapter review section is included at the end of each chapter.

Every chapter includes a "Your Turn" activity that allows you to practice the ideas you have learned.

The "Work with Me" sections will give you step-by step instructions on how to apply the material to your project. Work alongside the instructions on your computer to achieve a goal.

Many "Work with Me" and "Your Turn" activities will ask you to add new code, edit existing code, or remove old code. We will use a light gray color to represent old code and black text for new code. Any existing code that needs to be removed will be crossed out.

```
This line shows work that is already in the file
This black text shows the work you need to add.
This line shows another row of text that was already in the file.
Crossed out text needs to be removed.
```

What You Will Learn and Do In This Course

KidCoder[TM]*: Advanced Web Design* starts where the *KidCoder*[TM]*: Beginning Web Design* course left off. This course is written for 4th grade or higher school students who have an interest in building web sites. You will learn HTML5, CSS3, JavaScript, and other new features to make exciting and interactive web sites. You will also learn how to use a free program called Komodo Edit, which makes typing out code much easier.

Each lesson will include an explanation of concepts, examples of how concepts are used, and one or more activities that will help you understand the concept. Throughout the course, you will be challenged to apply what you have learned by building your own web site from scratch.

What You Need to Know Before Starting

You are expected to have a good understanding of the material in *KidCoder*[TM]*: Beginning Web Design*. If you have any questions about that course, please review the earlier topics before beginning this course.

You are expected to already know the basics of computer use before beginning this course. You need to know how to use the keyboard and mouse to select and run programs, use application menu systems, and work with either the Microsoft Windows or Apple Mac operating system. You should understand how to save and load files on your computer and how to use the Windows Explorer or Mac Finder to walk through your file system and directory structures. You should also have some experience with using text editors, like Notepad or TextEdit and web browsers, like Safari or Firefox.

Software Versions

You will be using the free, cross-platform *Komodo Edit* software to complete this course. You will be guided through the download and installation of this software during an early activity. You may also use *Microsoft Paint* or *Mac Preview/iPhoto* to create and edit graphics and images. These programs come shipped with your operating systems. All supplemental documents installed with the course material are in Adobe Acrobat (PDF) format. You must have the Adobe Acrobat Reader installed to view these documents.

Course Errata

We welcome your feedback regarding any course details that are unclear or that may need correction. You can find a list of course errata for this edition on our website.

Getting Help

Throughout the course you will be given some problem solving tips to help you find and fix problems. The earlier tips can be used to troubleshoot later exercises as well.

All courses come with a Solution Guide and fully coded solutions for all activities. Simply install the "Solution Files" from your course setup program and you can refer to the solutions as needed from the "Solution Menu". If you are confused about any activity, you can see how we solved the problem!

We also offer free technical support for students and teachers. Simply fill out the help request form in the "Support" area of our website with a detailed question and we will assist you.

Activity Starters

Some exercises and assignments require graphical images. We have provided all of those images for you in the "KidCoder/AdvancedWebDesign/Activity Starters" directory. In addition, a few activities may require a lot of typing to enter text content. To make your job easier, we have also provided text files in the "Activity Starters" directory containing this text content. You can cut and paste from the starter text files into your own code to save some time. Please look at the "Activity Starters" tab in your Student Menu for details on the starter material. When starter material is available, it will be noted in the activity description.

Support for Multiple Operating Systems

This course was developed for use both on Microsoft Windows and Apple Mac OS X operating systems. While HTML can be used on nearly any computer platform, our course setup program will only run on these systems, and we give guidance using the tools and terms specific Windows and Mac OS. We will point out in text or by screen shots any differences between the operating systems. Where necessary, we will provide dedicated sets of instructions for handling each operating system.

Directory Naming Conventions

On Windows systems, directory paths are traditionally represented with backslashes ("\") between folder names like this: **KidCoder\AdvancedWebDesign**. However, forward slashes ("/") also work. On Mac OS, directories use forward slashes as in **KidCoder/AdvancedWebDesign**. In order to avoid cluttering the textbook with both representations, each time we specify a path, we will simply use the forward slash ("/") style which works on both operating systems.

Chapter One: Getting Started

Welcome to the *KidCoder™: Advanced Web Design* course! In this course you will learn new HTML5, CSS3, and JavaScript skills to create more interesting and lively websites.

Please Run the Course Setup Program on Your Computer

If you have not already done so, please run the setup program that came with your course. Printed textbooks contain a "Course CD" in the back with the setup program. This setup program will install extra course material such as activity starters for the students or tests and solutions for the teacher. The Solution Files can be installed on a separate computer to keep them apart from the Student Files. Please refer to the "Getting Started Guide" document located in the Installation area of our website, www.HomeschoolProgramming.com, for additional information on how to run the setup program. The latest installation updates for this course are under the "Installing KidCoder Web" tab on our website.

Once the course material is installed on your computer, you will have shortcuts to an "Advanced Web Student Menu" and/or "Advanced Web Solution Menu" in your Windows Start menu or Mac OS user directory. The Student Menu contains links to things for a student such as activity starters or other supplemental instructions. The Solution Menu contains a Solution Guide and fully coded activity solutions for the teacher, so if you ever get stuck on a problem you can always check to see how we solved it.

Windows (up to 7) Course Menu Shortcuts

On a Windows 7 or earlier computers, once installation is complete you will have a new "KidCoder" group on your Windows Start Menu. Underneath "KidCoder" is an "Advanced Web Design" folder. Within that folder are the Student and Solution Menus (depending on your choices during setup). The look and feel of the Windows Start Menu may change between versions of Windows, but your final menu system should look something like the image to the right (assuming both Student and Solution files were installed).

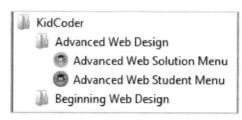

Windows 8 Menu Shortcuts

Because Windows 8 does not have an easy Start menu, after installation you may want to "pin" the menu shortcuts to your Start screen. To do this, first find the shortcuts by typing "Advanced Web" on your Start screen. You should see the shortcuts for your course appear on the screen.

To pin these shortcuts to the Start screen, just right-click on the shortcut and choose "Pin to Start" from the menu at the bottom of your screen. You can also follow this procedure later when you install Komodo Edit or any other 3rd party software that you want to pin to your Start screen.

Pin to Start

Open file location

Mac OS Course Menu Shortcuts

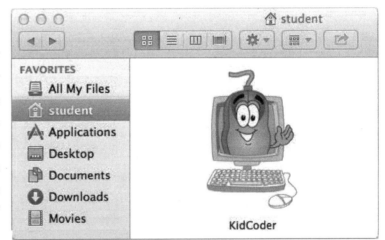

Once the installation is completed on your Mac OS computer, you will see a new "KidCoder" image in your user's Home folder. When you double-click on this image, you will see the "Advanced Web Design" folder and the links to the "Advanced Web Student Menu" and the "Advanced Web Solution Menu" (depending on your choices during setup).

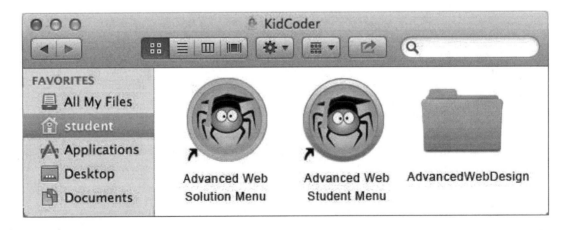

Your "MyProjects" Folder

The setup program automatically created the "/KidCoder/AdvancedWebDesign" directory, and inside you will find an empty "MyProjects" folder. We recommend placing all of your web projects inside sub-folders within "MyProjects". If more than one student wants to create projects at the same time, you can use Windows Explorer or Mac OS Finder to create more project directories on your own. That way each student can work in a separate directory.

Lesson One: What You Already Know

You should have already completed the introductory *KidCoder*^{TM}*: Beginning Web Design* course. That course began teaching you web design, HTML and CSS syntax. Without a good understanding of the first course, you will have difficulty completing the advanced web design lessons.

In this lesson we will review some key web design ideas and the HTML and CSS that you have already learned. If you are not comfortable with any of these topics, we recommend you review the *KidCoder*^{TM}*: Beginning Web Design* material first before continuing with the advanced lessons!

 This lesson is just a brief review of the concepts that you learned in the *KidCoder*^{TM}*: Beginning Web Design* course. You should know these concepts before attempting the *KidCoder*^{TM}*: Advanced Web Design* course.

How the Internet Works

The Internet is made up of may connected computers. Some computers are **servers**, which means they contain information that other computers need. All servers have a unique domain name such as "homeschoolprogramming.com". This domain name is part of the URL (Uniform Resource Locator) used to access specific data on a server. A common URL will contain the protocol like "http", the domain name, and an optional resource such as a file in a directory.

http://www.homeschoolprogramming.com/index.php

For this course we are not using a server. Instead your HTML pages will live directly on your hard drive, and the URL you enter into your web browser will start with "file" instead of "http":

file:///C:/KidCoder/AdvancedWebDesign/MyProjects/Aquamaniacs/index.html

Files and Directories on your Hard Drive

A **file** is a named collection of data on your hard drive. HTML pages containing web content, like "index.html", are one type of file. The file extension (the part after the period) gives some hints as to what the file contains. All files are stored in a **directory** or **folder**. Folders can be arranged in nested groups where a parent folder can contain one or more child folders. When writing out these folder names, they are separated by a slash like this: "parent folder/child folder". You can use a **relative** path from your current location to reach another folder, or you can create an **absolute** path from the root directory.

Using Text Editors

HTML files contain plain text, so you can create and edit HTML files with any of the simple text editors that come pre-installed with your operating system. You should be familiar with using Notepad on Windows or TextEdit on Mac OS to create, modify, and save text files.

HTML Elements

An HTML **element** starts with an opening angle bracket "<", then the element name such as "p" for paragraph, then a closing angle bracket ">". After this opening tag comes any data or other elements that belong inside. An element is closed with an angle bracket "<", forward slash "/", the element name, and the closing angle bracket ">".

```
<p>This line is within a paragraph.</p>
```

Elements may optionally hold **attributes** after the opening element name. Attributes are name-value pairs that help style or describe the element.

```
<p style="font-size:20px">This line is within a paragraph.</p>
```

HTML File Layout

A normal HTML file will contain three main elements. The **<html>** element is the outermost element containing all other mark-up and data. The **<head>** element contains meta-data, or information about the page such as key words and title. But the **<head>** element does not contain any data visible in the main content area of the web browser.

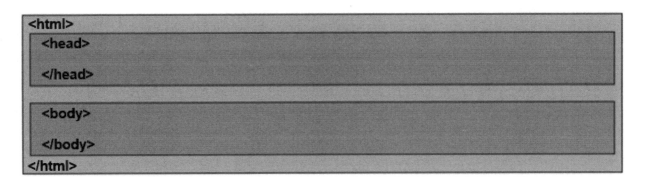

The **<!DOCTYPE>** declaration found at the very top tells the browser what version of HTML is in the file. This is the only element above the **<html>** element.

Header Elements

In the <**head**> element you will find <**meta**> elements describing the web page. You can also add a <**title**> element that contains a brief text description of the web page. The title will be shown at the very top of the web browser and possibly in other locations depending on the browser and operating system. If you are using external CSS stylesheets, the <**link**> element will set the path to those sheets.

Body Elements

Text, pictures, and other content found within the <**body**> element are displayed in the main part of the web browser. The appearance of this content (such as color or size) can be adjusted by adding HTML elements or styles. Some common HTML elements are listed in the table below.

<a>	Hyperlink (anchor) to another web page, or another location in this web page
<blockquote>	Sets the content off as a quotation from another source
** **	Adds a line break at this location
<div>	Creates a logical section on a web page that can be styled later.
<em>	Emphasizes content with *italics*
<h1>	Creates a primary headline. Smaller headlines use <h2>, <h3>, etc.
<img>	Adds an image or photograph to the page
<ol> and <ul>	Creates an ordered or unordered list with numbers or bullets
<p>	Creates a paragraph on the page
<strong>	Makes the content stand out in **bold**-face.
<table>	Creates a table of information with rows and data cells.

CSS

Cascading Style Sheets (CSS) are a powerful tool for setting the look and feel of a web page or entire website. You can use **inline** CSS to style a particular element within a page. To do this, add a `style` attribute with the style declaration as the value.

```
<p style="font-size:20px">This line is within a paragraph.</p>
```

If you want to apply styles to all elements on a page, you can move the style information up into the <**head**> area within a new <**style**> element.

```
<style type="text/css">
p {
font-size: 20px;
}
</style>
</head>
```

The text before each opening curly brace is the **selector**. The selector controls or selects the elements to which the style will apply. In this example, all paragraph <**p**> elements will be selected.

The most powerful use of CSS comes with external CSS, where you place your style declarations in one or more separate files. Then you can link multiple HTML pages to a central set of styles, and every web page on your site will automatically adjust its appearance based on these shared styles.

```
@charset "utf-8";
p {
font-size: 20px;
}
```

Choosing Colors

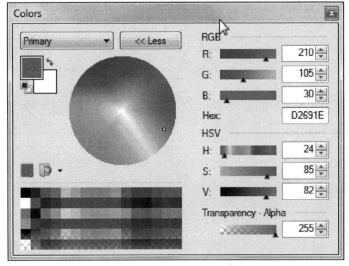

Colors on web pages are set with a combination of Red, Green, and Blue values. This RGB color system most commonly uses values in hexadecimal format, which begins with a pound sign # followed by 6 digits. Each digit is a value in the range 0, 1, 2, 3, 4, 5, 6, 7, 8, 9, A, B, C, D, E, F. A pair of digits can represent a decimal value between 0 (#00) and 255 (#FF). The full six-digit color contains the red values first, then the green, and then the blue. For example, #D2691E has #D2 for red, #69 for green, and #1E for blue, and these values combined create a "chocolate" color. You can also use many common color names such as "aqua", "white", or "pink".

Styling Text

You can apply many styles to control the appearance of text on a web page. A **font** is a collection of characters drawn in a certain style such as "Times New Roman", "Courier New", or "Arial". You can set the font size, **weight**, color, background color, margins and padding, and other properties.

Styling by ID and Class

You can give individual elements unique names with the "**id**" attribute. Or, you can add the same "**class**" attribute to one or more elements on the page.

```
<p id="first">This is the only first paragraph.</p>
<p class="main">This is one main paragraph.</p>
<p class="main">This is another main paragraph.</p>
```

Either way, you can then apply styles to the elements by **id** or **class**. To apply a style to an id, use the pound sign # in front of the id name as the selector. To apply a style to a class, use a period (.) in front of the class name.

```
#first {
}
.main {
}
```

Styling Hyperlinks

You can apply normal text styles and borders to anchor <**a**> elements. You can also change the link style based on whether or not the user has visited it before and what the user might be doing with the mouse cursor over the ink. The selectors "**a:link**", "**a:hover**", "**a:visited**", and "**a:active**" will apply to the link in its default state, while the user is hovering the mouse cursor over the link, when the link has already been visited, or when the use is actively clicking down on the link.

Styling Borders

Borders are lines around the edges of elements. You can control the border size, style, and color on the entire element or on individual top, bottom, left, and right sides.

```
p {
border-width: 3px;
border-style: solid;
border-color: blue;
}
```

```
Look at my paragraph borders!
```

Background Images

Images add visual interest to your web page. You can add images as backgrounds to other elements using the **background-image** property. Or, you can add images as content within the page using the **<img>** element. Either way, be sure to prepare your image for web use with proper editing. You can crop the image to a smaller area, compress it to a smaller size, and convert it to a format recognized by all web browsers.

Tables

It's easy to display data in a grid using the **<table>** element. Within the table you will have **<tr>** rows, **<th>** header cells, and **<td>** data cells. Each type of cell can be styled differently, and you can also add borders in between each cell.

	Sweep	Dishes	Trash
Joe	Mon	Wed	Fri
Sally	Tues	Thurs	Sat

Other Topics

We've quickly reviewed the major topics you already learned in your first-semester class. But we haven't mentioned every subject! You also learned about things like relative and absolute positioning, layering, changing the mouse cursor, and creating custom list bullets. We spent some time learning how to plan a website with a site map and create and link together sub-pages. We also reviewed the rules for cascading styles in detail. Having a good understanding of the cascading rules will be very important in this class! You will learn more advanced ways to select and apply cascading styles to specific elements on a web page.

Lesson Two: Web Editing Tools

To get the best results from this course, you use a recent version of your preferred web browser. Some of the assignments will use features of HTML5 and CSS3 that are only supported on web browsers released within the last year or two. This is particularly important for Internet Explorer users, because Internet Explorer didn't start supporting most of the HTML5 tags until IE9, with the best support occurring in versions IE10 and later.

You will get a chance to study your web browser version and HTML5 / CSS3 compatibility in a later lesson.

Web Editing Tools

We know the Internet is here to stay, and there is money to be made in web site design. For this reason, people have developed some amazing tools to make this process as simple and painless as possible. The most popular tools used by professional web designers are programs called "Adobe Dreamweaver" and "Microsoft FrontPage". These programs contain WYSIWYG (What You See Is What You Get) tools as well as the ability to directly edit the HTML code. They offer automatic links, link checking, drag-and-drop tools, helpful debugging features and great file management abilities. Unfortunately, both programs are very expensive! This means that they are not a great option for new web designers.

Text Editors vs. Code Editors

You should be familiar with text editor software like Notepad and TextEdit. These programs are designed to help you create text documents on your computer. A *code editor*, on the other hand is a text editor that goes one step further – giving you some extra functionality that simplifies and speeds up the input and editing of source code. Code editors will often highlight variables, point out syntax errors, and offer debugging tools for your source code. A really good code editor will be able to handle a variety of programming languages and will contain drag-and-drop toolboxes for code snippets and common elements.

Komodo Edit

In *KidCoder™: Beginning Web Design* you used a basic text editor (Notepad or TextEdit) to create your web site. In this course, you will learn about *Komodo Edit*, a popular, free code editor and web design software that works on the Windows, Mac and Linux operating systems. It can be used to write web sites or create programs in other programming languages. It has the ability to check syntax, highlight code, and search for key words. Komodo Edit also provides a drag-and-drop tool box as well as an on-demand preview screen so you can see how your web site looks without having to open it up in a browser program.

Komodo Edit may release new versions from time to time. You can usually install the latest version without having to worry about matching the exact version described in our lessons. Please see our website under the "Installing KidCoder Web" area for any updated instructions.

> We are going to spend some time exploring Komodo Edit features in the next lesson and will assume you are using Komodo Edit in the activity descriptions. However, you can complete the entire course using a simple text editor if you prefer not to use Komodo Edit for any reason!

 **Your Turn Activity: Installing Komodo Edit**

In this activity you will download and install the Komodo Edit software on your computer.

Your activity requirements and instructions are found in the "Chapter_01_Activity1.pdf" document located in your "KidCoder/AdvancedWebDesign/Activity Docs" folder. You can access this document through your Student Menu or by double-clicking on it from Windows Explorer or Mac OS Finder.

Complete this activity now and ensure you understand the material before continuing!

Lesson Three: Komodo Edit Projects

We are going to use Komodo Edit as the web design tool for the rest of this course, though you can choose to use a simple text editor if you prefer. To start this software on Windows 7 or earlier, click on the Start menu and look for the "ActiveState Komodo Edit" folder. You should find the link for the "Komodo Edit 8" program in that folder as shown to the right.

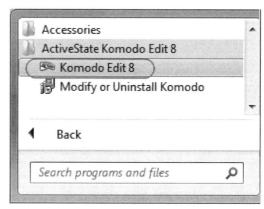

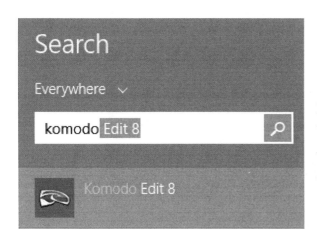

In Windows 8, you can find your Komodo Edit program by typing "Komodo Edit" while on the Start screen. If you want to keep this icon on your Start screen, you can right-click the icon and choose "Pin to Start" from the menu.

If you are using a Mac computer, you can find the "Komodo Edit 8" program in your Applications folder as shown below:

Once the program opens, you should see the Komodo Edit "Start Page". This page is mostly a bulletin board for ActiveState Software and Komodo Edit. "What's new" tells you about Komodo Edit and often has some marketing on it. "Quick Links" are shortcuts to some tools and "Recent Projects and Files" will show what you have worked on recently.

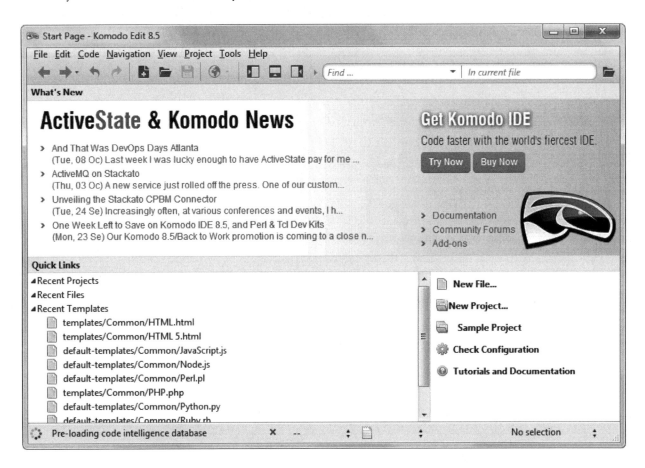

Seeing the Start Page appear every time you open Komodo Edit can be annoying. Fortunately, Komodo Edit gives you the freedom to make the program screen look the way you want by setting your preferences. You can decide how to lay out your work area, enable auto-completion of your code, and even allow you to decide what colors you want to use to highlight your code. You will explore this area more once you get to know how the program works. For now, we will mostly stick to the default settings for the program. The one setting that you can change right now, however, is turning off the start page.

 **Work with Me: Turning off the Komodo Start Page**

You may want to turn off the Start Page every time you start the Komodo Edit program. Here are instructions for turning off this feature:

Instructions

1. Under the main navigation bar, select "Edit → Preferences".
2. Under the "Appearance" category, uncheck "Show Komodo Start Page on startup".
3. Click on "OK" to save your changes.

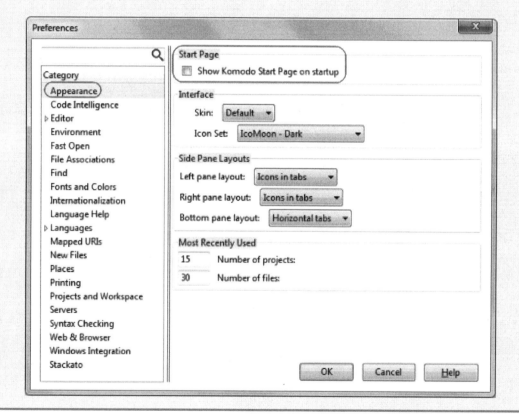

Exploring the Komodo Edit IDE

The screen shot on the next page shows a typical Komodo Edit IDE with a project that already has several web pages. Your own program may look a bit different on a different version of Windows or Mac OS. We've added some circled numbers in each main area for easy reference.

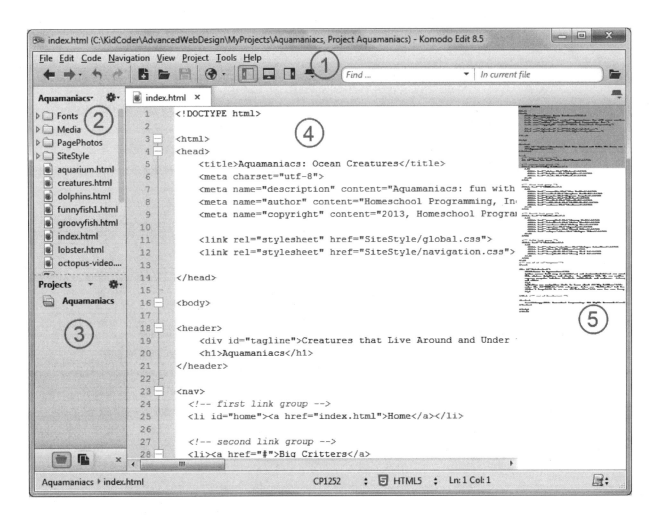

The first area (1) contains a program menu and toolbar that lets you access all Komodo Edit commands and features. The second area (2) shows the files and folders belonging to the project you have loaded. The third area (3) contains a list of recent projects that you have opened. Since we'll be working mostly with one project in this course, you can make that "Projects" panel as small as possible.

The fourth area (4) contains a tabbed list of text files (HTML, CSS, JavaScript) that you have opened for editing. This area is a full-featured text editor with color highlighting of HTML syntax and other nice features you'll discover over time. The fifth area (5) shows a "mini-map" with a birds-eye view of the current source file. You can use the mini-map to quickly scroll around large files, or right-click on the map and hide it if you don't want to see it.

Projects

So what exactly is a "project" in Komodo Edit? Basically a project is your website, including all of the files and folders inside your root directory. Komodo Edit gives you an easy way to quickly manage and edit all of these website pieces without moving back and forth to Windows Explorer or Mac OS Finder. The project panel in the top left can be used just like Explorer or Finder for many tasks such as creating directories or moving and renaming files.

Komodo Edit will create a file called "<project name>.komodoproject" inside your web site's root directory. This file contains some project settings and other information. You should never have to edit or look inside this file. But if you see it on your hard drive, you'll know you have created a Komodo Edit project in that directory. You can double-click that file to load your project into Komodo Edit. You may also see a ".komodotools" directory that contains internal settings you don't have to worry about.

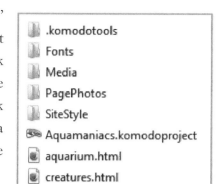

Introducing Aquamaniacs

Throughout this course you are going to be building a website about the different creatures that live in and around the ocean. This new website will be called "Aquamaniacs!"

We'll start off very simply and then make the website more complex as you learn new skills.

The Aquamaniacs web site is going to be much larger than the Raptors site that you built in the *KidCoder*^{TM}: *Beginning Web Design* course. We will be building the Aquamaniacs site in stages, with each new lesson adding onto the previous one.

Work with Me: Creating the Aquamaniacs Project

To get started with Komodo Edit, we need to create our first project!

1. Using Windows Explorer or Mac OS Finder, create a new folder under your "KidCoder/AdvancedWebDesign/MyProjects" directory called "Aquamaniacs". We will use this folder to hold our web site for this course. These two pictures show the Explorer and Finder results after you have created your new folder.

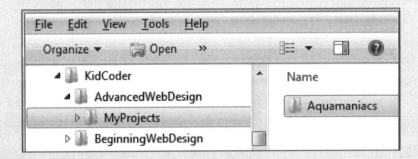

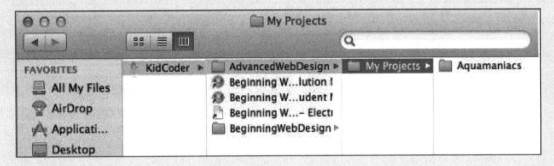

2. Open your Komodo Edit software and create a new Aquamaniacs project in that folder. To do this, from the menu along the top of the page, select "Project → New Project" from the drop-down list.

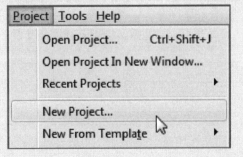

3. In the "New Project" screen, browse to your project folder under "MyProjects":

   "/KidCoder/AdvancedWebDesign/MyProjects/Aquamaniacs"

   Type in the file name "**Aquamaniacs.komodoproject**" and "Save" the project.

4. Now you have an empty Aquamaniacs project in Komodo Edit, like this:

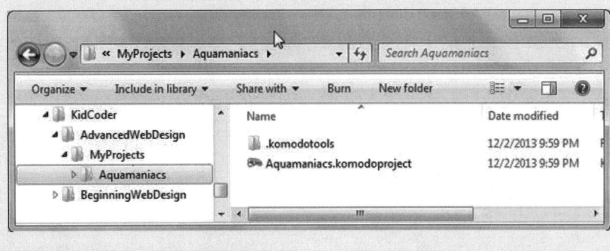

5. Let's take a look at what was created in your Aquamaniacs folder. The images below show Windows Explorer and Mac OS Finder views into the Aquamaniacs directory.

As you can see, we only have one file in our folder right now. This is the "project" file that contains the Komodo information about our Aquamaniacs project. You'll see more files appear in this folder as we continue adding new pages throughout the course.

Creating Pages with Komodo Edit

Creating web pages with Komodo Edit is really easy! In fact, you can have Komodo Edit create pages that already contain the common HTML elements for a web page. This is done using a concept called "templates". Templates are files that contain the basic structure for new files or projects. Komodo includes templates for a number of languages, but for now, we will be using the HTML5 template.

The HTML5 template will create a new file that already contains the HTML5 doctype, **<html>**, **<head>**, **<title>** and **<body>** tags. The **<!DOCTYPE>** tag will contain the proper doctype for an HTML5 document and the **<title>** tag will contain a default title value, like "Page Title". The other tags will be empty – just waiting for you to fill in the details!

Work with Me: Creating Aquamaniacs Home Page

Now we can create our "index.html" home page for our Aquamaniacs website using the HTML5 template in your Komodo Edit software. We'll discuss HTML5 in more detail in the next chapter.

1. First, we will use Komodo Edit to create a new file from a template. To do this, click on "File → New → File From Template". Make sure you do NOT click on "New File"!

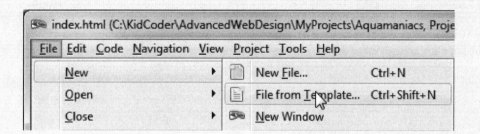

2. Next, you will see a list of "Categories" of templates. Select "Common" or "Web" and then find the "HTML 5" template in the list on the right of the screen.

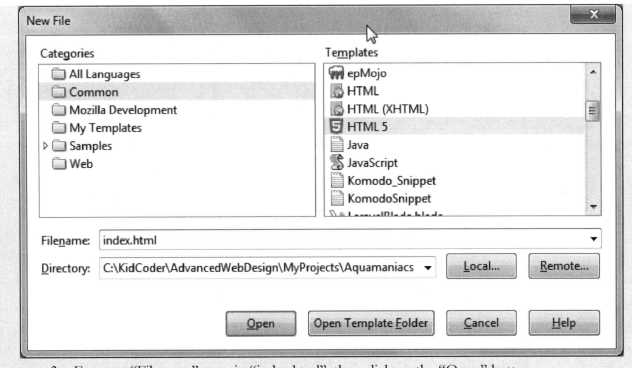

3. For your "Filename", type in "index.html", then click on the "Open" button.

4. Presto…Your home page is instantly created!

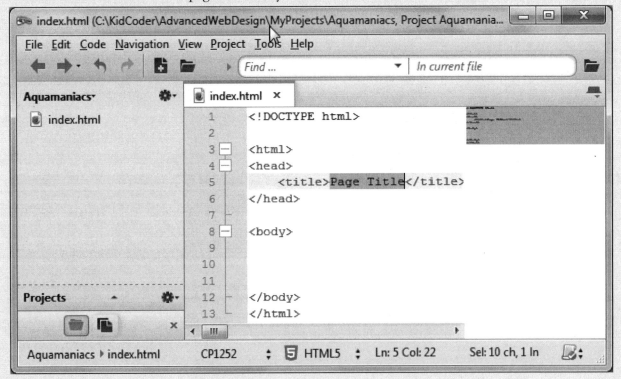

You can see the "index.html" file appear in your project panel to the left, and double-clicking on that file will bring it up in the center editing area.

Previewing Pages with Komodo Edit

One time-saving feature in Komodo Edit is the ability to preview a web page with the "Preview in Browser" feature. This feature will automatically display your page in a separate window, in the Editor Pane, or in a split view of the Editor Pane, depending on your preference settings.

 The "Preview in Browser" feature is only available when the "source" tab is in focus and you are viewing a supported file type (like an HTML file). If you are unable to choose this option, make sure you have clicked inside your HTML source file first!

To preview a file with the Preview in Browser feature:

1. Open the file in the Komodo Editor Pane. Or, if the file is already open, make sure it is the selected tab in the center editor area.
2. Select "View → Preview in Browser" from the menu. A dialog box will appear, prompting you to choose which file to preview.
3. If you want to preview the current file, select **Preview with this file**, or, if you want to preview using another file that includes the current file (use an HTML file to preview a CSS file), select **Preview with another file or URL**, then click **Browse** to navigate to the desired file location. If you do not want to be prompted each time you preview a specific file, select **Remember this selection for this file**.
4. Click **Preview**. The file will be displayed in the Editor Pane or in a separate window, depending on which preference you have chosen.

Of course there is no substitute for testing your web pages in one or more real web browsers! In most of our activity descriptions we'll ask you to reload your changes into your favorite web browser to see the results. But you are welcome to use the Komodo Edit preview feature to help test your work.

Work with Me: Komodo Edit Browser Preview

Let's use Komodo Edit's "Browser Preview" functionality to take a look at our new index.html page.

Instructions

1. The first step is to make sure your "index.html" file is open in an Edit window in Komodo Edit. The Browser Preview is not available unless you have a file open that you can preview.

2. Make sure that your "index.html" window has the focus. To do this, just place your cursor anywhere inside the text for that file.

3. Now click on "View → Browser Preview" from the top menu. (Windows example shown)

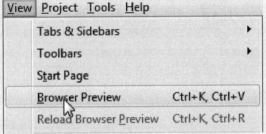

4. On the next window, pick "In a Komodo tab" and check "Remember this selection for this file" and then click on the "Preview" button. (Mac OS example shown)

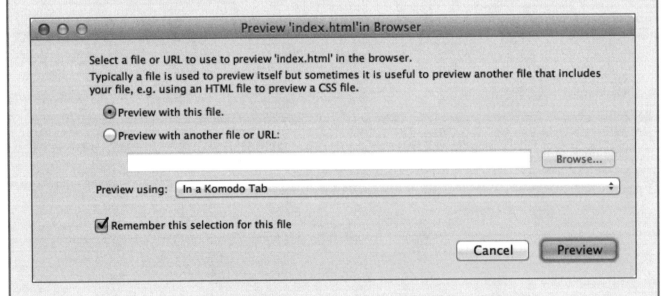

5. At this point, you should see the preview pane (shown at the bottom of the screen) with an empty body and a title reading "Page Title" in the tab.

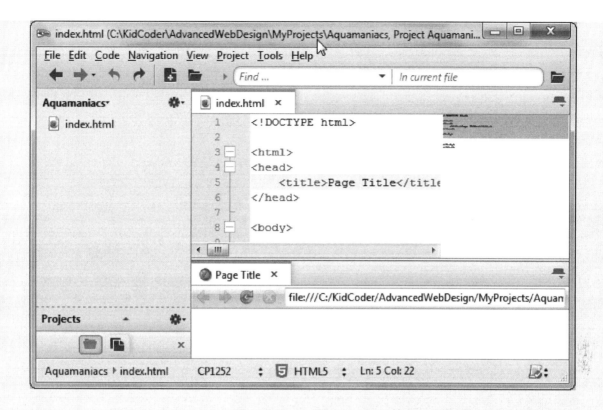

6. Now let's see how the preview changes to match code changes in our HTML file. In the "index.html" code pane, change the **<title>** element from "Page Title" to "Aquamaniacs: Ocean Creatures".

7. Once you have made your change, save your file. The bottom preview tab will automatically update to match your changes.

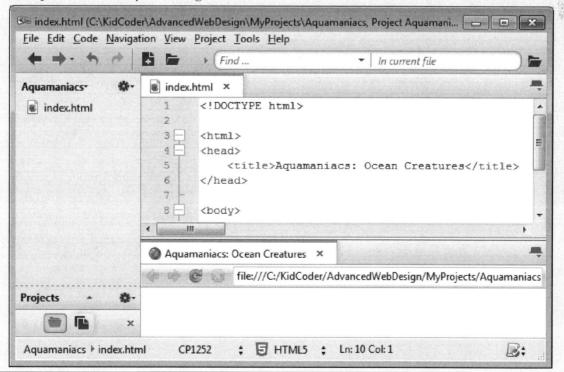

Chapter Review

- An HTML **element** starts with an opening angle bracket "<", then the element name such as "p" for paragraph, then a closing angle bracket ">".
- A normal HTML file will contain three main elements: **<html>**, **<head>** and **<body>**.
- Text, pictures, and other content in the **<body>** are shown in the main web browser screen.
- Cascading Style Sheets (CSS) can set the look and feel of a web page or entire website.
- CSS rules can be written inline with a **style** attribute inside an element tag, or as **<style>** information listed in the **<head>** section, or as external CSS located in a separate file.
- A **font** is a collection of characters drawn in a certain style.
- You can use images as backgrounds on other elements using the **background-image** property.
- You can give individual elements unique names with the "**id**" attribute.
- You can add the same "**class**" attribute to one or more elements on the page.
- In this course, we will be using the free Komodo Edit web design software and code editor.
- A *code editor* is a text editor that simplifies and speeds up the writing and editing of source code.
- A Komodo Edit project includes all of the files and folders inside your root directory.
- You can preview a website right in Komodo Edit using the "Preview in Browser" feature.

Your Turn Activity: Laying Out the Aquamaniacs Home page

In this activity you are going to set up the major areas of the Aquamaniacs home page based on the HTML skills you already have. The Aquamaniacs home page will have a header, footer, navigation bar, and main content area.

Your activity requirements and instructions are found in the "Chapter_01_Activity2.pdf" document located in your "KidCoder/AdvancedWebDesign/Activity Docs" folder. You can access this document through your Student Menu or by double-clicking on it from Windows Explorer or Mac OS Finder.

Complete this activity now and ensure you understand the material before continuing!

Chapter Two: Introducing HTML5

In the *KidCoder™: Beginner Web Design* course, you learned how to make a web site based on XHTML. Everything you learned in the basic course is still valid and makes a very solid web site. In this course you will learn how to use some of the newer features in HTML5 to improve and simplify your website.

Lesson One: HTML5 and Web Browsers

A group of smart web designers formed the **World Wide Web Consortium (W3C)** to help define the rules and standards for web mark-up. In our last course, we used a mark-up standard called XHTML, which was created by the W3C in 2000. In this course, we will use the latest standard, called HTML5. This new standard was the joint work of the W3C group and a new group called the **WHATWG (Web Hypertext Application Technology Working Group)**. This new group is composed mostly of browser companies, like Apple, Mozilla and Opera.

Goals of HTML5

The people developing HTML5 have a long list of challenging goals. Here are some important ideas:

- HTML5 should be **backward compatible**, meaning the new HTML5 code will work right alongside older versions of HTML.

- HTML5 should clearly define **error handling**, so browsers and adaptive software know how to act if there is an error on the web page.

- HTML5 should **simplify** markup. Many of the new HTML5 tags are simpler than they have been in the past. Simplified HTML5 mark-up makes web pages easier to write, use and access.

- HTML5 should support **accessibility**. HTML5 pages should be easier to read and process for both humans and computers, especially for people with disabilities.

- HTML5 should reduce the need for **third-party software**. Earlier versions of HTML need third-party plug-ins such as Flash or Silverlight to add features like multimedia support. HTML5 browsers will support multimedia and other features without any 3rd party plug-ins.

- Finally, HTML5 is using a more **casual or relaxed** syntax. In HTML5, you can use lowercase, uppercase, or mixed-case tag names or attributes on your web page. You can also use either quoted or unquoted values. Web browsers are expected to correctly process your HTML5 code, even if you don't follow strict XHTML rules for naming and syntax.

> **In HTML5, the letter cases don't matter, so these are all valid ways to create an HTML element:**
>
> - <html> </html>
> - <HTML> </HTML>
> - <Html> </Html>
> - <HtMl> <HtMl>

Many people believe these looser rules mean new web pages will become messy and sloppy, and they could be right. Other people think good designers have already developed good habits and they will continue to write clean, consistent code even if they don't have to.

Best Practice

It is **best practice** to follow some guidelines in writing your mark up so your page is consistent, easy to read, easy to maintain, and professional-looking. The following best practices are recommended.

- Use lowercase for all elements and attributes like you did in XHTML
- Use closing tags to end elements, even if not required
- Put quotation marks around all attribute values, even if not required
- Use indentations and line breaks to make your markup and code easier to read

Have you been wondering why you didn't just learn HTML5 right at the start? Now that you know how to follow strict XHTML rules to write clean code, you are going to be more successful in a casual HTML5 setting. You don't have to follow all of the old XHTML rules, but you can continue to use the good habits and best practices you already know.

Is HTML5 Complete?

HTML5 is not complete. But it is a very big standard, and many parts are already stable enough to be supported in all the major web browsers. However, caution is still needed! Although some HTML5 will work on most browsers, other parts are still unstable or not supported everywhere. This means that the code will work on some browsers, but not on others. We will focus on those parts that seem to be very stable and work well across most browsers.

Browsers that Support HTML5

Since HTML5 is not finished, no browsers on the market today will have full HTML5 support. However, you will find that the most browsers support the most common features of HTML5. Browsers are always working to add more support with each new release of the browser software.

How do you know how well your browser works with HTML5? The easiest way to go to a website called http://html5test.com. This website will look at your current browser and will tell you exactly what features of HTML5 are supported or not supported. Simply visiting the main page will automatically display a score.

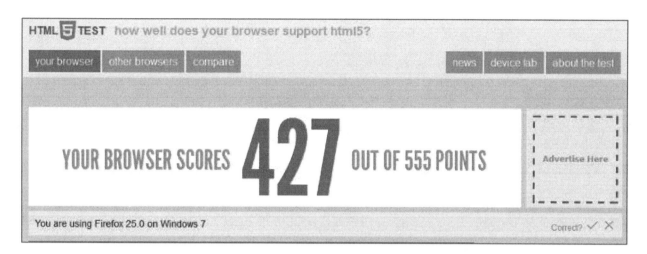

The website will also give you detailed information on exactly what parts of HTML5 your browser supports.

This is great information for any website designer, allowing you to easily see which HTML5 features are safe to use.

If you are curious how all major browsers compare, you can click on the "other browsers" tab at the top of the http://html5test.com page. The chart will list scores for other browsers.

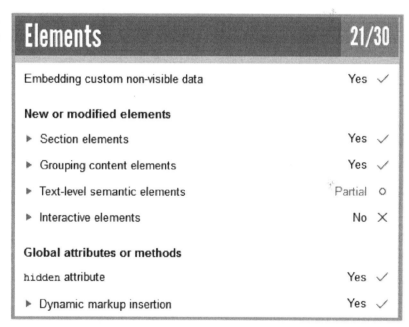

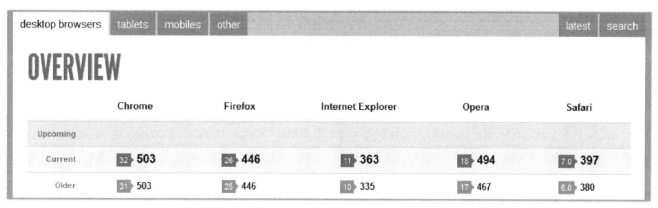

Minimum Browser for this Course

What browser should you use for this course? We are covering material that works on recent versions of Internet Explorer, Mozilla Firefox, Google Chrome, and Apple Safari. You should be using one of those major browsers. In order to complete all of the course activities successfully, your browser must be upgraded to at least the minimum version shown below for your software:

- Internet Explorer, version 10
- Mozilla Firefox, version 25
- Google Chrome, version 31
- Apple Safari, version 7

You can usually find the current version of your web browser by selecting "Help → About" or similar option from the web browser's menu. If your browser does not meet the minimum versions listed above, please upgrade it (with parent or teacher assistance) to the current version before continuing.

 **Work with Me: Verify Your Web Browser**

Let's inspect the web browser you will be using for this class. We'll need to make sure it can handle our HTML5 code!

1. Open the web browser software you will be using on your computer.
2. Find the web browser version by selecting "Help → About" or similar menu option from the browser menu. Is it equal to or greater than the minimum version listed above?
3. Next, visit the "html5test" website to see your browser's score. Enter the address http://html5test.com to get your score.
4. Does your browser score in the upper 300s or above?
5. If your browser does not match one of our listed minimum versions, take some time with parent or teacher assistance and upgrade the browser to the latest version now!

Lesson Two: Identifying HTML5 Pages

One of the main HTML5 goals is to simply mark-up. Earlier HTML elements were reviewed to see if they could be made easier for humans and browsers to manage. In this lesson we are going to review the top-level HTML elements that identify a web page to see how they have changed in HTML5.

The <!DOCTYPE> Element

<!DOCTYPE> was important in XHTML to state exactly which kind of mark-up was used by the page. In HTML5, this element simply says that the file contains a web page, and it does not state the exact version of the HTML code inside.

XHTML	<!DOCTYPE html PUBLIC "-//W3C//DTD XHTML 1.0 Strict//EN" "http://www.w3.org/TR/xhtml1/DTD/xhtml1-strict.dtd">
HTML5	<!DOCTYPE html>

The <!**DOCTYPE**> is still needed at the top of your page, but you don't need all the extra stuff that came with the XHTML version. Notice the new version states "html" and not "html5". Web browsers have to support all existing versions of HTML on the web, plus HTML5, plus any new versions that come out in the future. So the tag simply states "html" and lets the browser figure out the details based on what it finds inside the code. The new tag is simple and easy to remember.

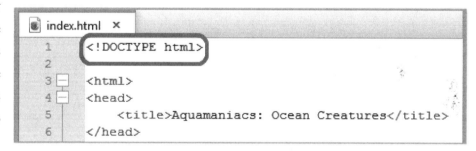

The <html> Element

The HTML element (**<html>**) is also much simpler in HTML5. In fact, you can simply use the **<html>** tag by itself. Many web site designers will also add the optional attribute **lang** that tells the browser the main language for the web page. The value of "*en*" tells the browser the page is in English. If you have a French page, you would use "**<html lang="fr">**", or a Spanish page would use "**<html lang="es">**". You can find thousands of other language abbreviations online.

XHTML	<html xmlns="http://www.w3.org/1999/xhtml">
HTML5	<html> <html lang="en">

The <link> Element

In the stylesheet <**link**> element, the attribute **type**="**text/css**" was used to tell the browser that the style sheet will be a text file containing CSS. However, this value is not really necessary since style sheets are ALWAYS text/css files. HTML5 just assumes the type is the "text/css", making the links to style sheets shorter and easier.

XHTML	<link href="SiteStyle/global.css" rel="stylesheet" type="text/css" />
HTML5	<link href="SiteStyle/global.css" rel="stylesheet">

Closing Tags

In XHTML, every self-closing element without any content was ended with a self-closing slash (/>). You can still use that style in HTML5, but it is no longer required. Your self-closing elements can skip the closing "/" and just use ">". A good example of this change is found in the <**meta**> and <**br**> tags.

XHTML	<meta name="author" content="Silly Sally" />
HTML5	<meta name="author" content="Silly Sally">

Character Set

Character encoding is an optional, but highly recommended <**meta**> tag for HTML5 web pages. The format is simpler but still tells the browser what kind of character set is used in the rest of the page. This element should go at the very beginning of the <**head**> area before any other elements like <**title**>.

XHTML	<meta http-equiv="Content-Type" content="text/html;charset=utf-8" />
HTML5	<meta charset="utf-8">

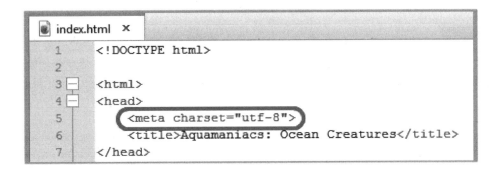

```
index.html  ✕
1    <!DOCTYPE html>
2
3    <html>
4    <head>
5        <meta charset="utf-8">
6        <title>Aquamaniacs: Ocean Creatures</title>
7    </head>
```

Work with Me: Adding HTML5 Meta Tags to the Home Page

Let's spend a few minutes to add the HTML5 <**meta**> tags to our Aquamaniacs "index.html" page.

1. Load "index.html" in Komodo Edit and move your cursor down just inside the <**head**> element.
2. Type in the first <**meta**> line with charset information shown below. Komodo Edit may give you some drop-down tools or automatically complete your statement to be helpful.
3. Then move below the <**title**> element and add the other <**meta**> statements shown below.

```
<head>
    <meta charset="utf-8">
    <title>Aquamaniacs: Ocean Creatures</title>
    <meta name="description" content="Aquamaniacs: fun with ocean creatures.">
    <meta name="author" content="Homeschool Programming, Inc.">
    <meta name="copyright" content="2013, Homeschool Programming">
</head>
```

4. Save your changes to "index.html" and reload the file in a web browser. You should not see any visible changes, but now your page is properly described with HTML5 <**meta**> information.

The <head>, <title> and <body> Elements

The <**head**>, <**title**>, and <**body**> elements are exactly the same in HTML5. The <**head**> is the "brain" of the page. This area contains information about the page and instructions for the browser, but is not visible to people viewing the page in the browser. The <**title**> should contain a short description of the page is always found between the <**head**> and </**head**> tags. The words you use in a title will show up along the title bar of your browser, in the taskbar at the bottom of the computer screen, and as a bookmark label. The <**body**> of the web page contains everything you see on the screen such as headings, paragraphs, images, navigation and footers.

```
<html>
<head>
    <meta charset="utf-8">
    <title>Aquamaniacs: Ocean Creatures</title>
</head>

<body>


</body>
</html>
```

Lesson Three: HTML5 Element Updates

HTML5 elements for the most part look and work just like the "classic" HTML and XHTML elements you already know. However, HTML5 has made some changes. Some really old elements that used to be discouraged have been brought back and some existing elements have small changes.

Obsolete and Changed Elements

Whenever an existing HTML element or attribute is removed from a newer HTML standard, that element is labeled **deprecated** and designers are advised not to use them anymore. In fact, if they are used in a web page, there is no guarantee that browsers will be able to properly display the page.

Since HTML5 is trying to be backward compatible, the new browsers need to support the old elements, even if they are no longer used in HTML5. The new term for these old tags is **obsolete**. Obsolete elements are not recommended for use, but browsers must still support them.

Some deprecated elements have been brought back to recommended use by HTML5. HTML5 has also changed the way some existing elements work. We're going to review the most common changes to old or existing HTML elements in this lesson.

The <small> Element

The <small> element was used to make small text on a web page. This element was removed from use when CSS became the preferred method to control content size. The HTML5 standard says <small> is no longer a presentation element that sets a size, but instead is used to set aside legal content or content that should be written in fine print.

Classic HTML	<small>small sized text</small>
XHTML	<div style="font-size:small;" >small sized text</div>
HTML5	<small>small sized text</small>

The copyright at the bottom of a web page would be a good place to use the <small> element. The size of <small> is actually not defined, so you can use CSS to tell the browsers how you want it to look.

The <b> Element

The <b> or bold element was a commonly used tag in classic HTML web pages. It was simply used to create **bold** text. When CSS became available, it was replaced by the <**strong**> element. In HTML5, the designers decided to bring back the <**b**> tag. This tag is now used to create a unique visual style without implying extra importance.

Classic HTML	<b>bold text</b>
XHTML	<strong>bold text</strong>
HTML5	<strong>bold text</strong> <b>uniquely styled text</b>

Why do we still need the <**strong**> tag? The <**strong**> tag not only makes the visual text bold, but it lets a screen reader know to give that text extra emphasis. So use <**b**> if you just want a visual effect, or use <**strong**> if you want both visual effects and extra meaning for screen readers.

The <i> Element

The classic italics tag, <**i**>, was set aside in favor of the emphasis element <**em**> when CSS arrived. HTML5 has brought back the <**i**> element as a way to show text that has a different voice or mood. Browsers will probably show <**i**> mark-up in *italic* font, so use CSS styles to make it look the way you want.

Classic HTML	<i>italicized text</i>
XHTML	<em> italicized text </em>
HTML5	<em> italicized text </em> <i>text in a different voice or mood</i>

The difference between <**i**> and <**em**> is similar to <**b**> and <**strong**>. The <**i**> tag shows a different visual style only, while the <**em**> tag has a different visual style and has extra meaning for screen readers.

The <cite> Element

The <**cite**> element has been the subject of many debates in the web design community. In classic HTML the <**cite**> element was used around a person's name as the author or source for some quoted text. In HTML5 the <**cite**> element is meant to define the title of something and not the author. Since the best meaning of <**cite**> is still being discussed, you can decide for yourself how you want to use it on your site.

The Anchor (Link) <a> Element

The link element <a> has always been fundamental to web sites. However, in HTML5 its definition has been given a facelift. There are two main changes to how this element is now used:

- The **name** attribute is obsolete, so you should use the **id** attribute to create a page bookmark.
- The <a> element can now wrap around block elements and multiple elements if you want all of them to link to the same page. The only limitation is that you cannot nest an <a>element inside another <a>element.

XHTML	`<a href="whale.html"><h1>Whale Headline</h1></a>`
	`<a href="whale.html"><p>Description </p></a>`
	`<a href="whale.html"><img src="whale.png"/></a>`

HTML5	`<a href="whale.html">`
	`  <h1>Whale Headline</h1>`
	`  <p>Description</p>`
	`  <img src="whale.png">`
	`</a>`

The Line Break
 Element

The line break element forces a new line to begin. It has changed slightly in HTML5 – you do not need the space and trailing slash at the end anymore. Self-closing elements in HTML5 can skip the self-closing slash.

XHTML	` `
HTML5	` `

Shorthand Properties

Some properties like **margin** and **padding** have 4 separate parts such as **margin-top**, **margin-right**, **margin-bottom**, and **margin-left**. That's quite a bit of typing to set all 4 values, but fortunately there is a shorthand version to make your CSS rules easier.

This feature is not new to HTML5 or CSS3, and you will see it widely used on other websites. But we haven't talked about it before now, so we want to cover this important concept.

Instead of writing a line for each sub-property, you can string all the values together in a single line.

margin: *top right bottom left*;

padding: *top right bottom left*;

You can list from one to four values after the **margin** and **padding** properties. When four values are used, the first value always refers to the top margin, the second refers to the right margin, the third value is the bottom margin, and the fourth value is the left margin.

```
margin: 20px 30px 40px 50px;
        (top) (right) (bottom) (left)
```

If three values are used, they refer to the top margin first, then the right margin, and finally the bottom margin. The left margin is not set.

```
margin: 20px 30px 40px;
        (top) (right) (bottom)
```

If two values are used, the first value sets the top and bottom margins and the second value sets the right and left margins.

```
margin: 20px  30px;
        (top/bottom) (right/left)
```

When you only use one value, it assigns that value to all four margins.

```
margin: 20px;
        (ALL margins)
```

Similarly, the **background** property can be used to set the **background-color**, **background-position**, **background-size**, **background-repeat**, **background-image**, and other properties on a single line.

```
background: #FFFFFF left top 100px 50px url('my_image.png') no-repeat;
            (color)  (position)  (size)     (image)          (repeat)
```

Each of the individual properties above is optional and can be left out. Any property that is not present in the shortcut is set to its default value.

In addition to **margin**, **padding**, and **background**, other shortcuts exist for things like **border** and **font** styles. We will use shortcuts in our own examples, so don't be surprised when they appear.

Chapter Review

- HTML5 goals include: backward compatibility, better error handling, simplified mark-up, accessibility, less need for third-party software, and a more relaxed syntax.

- It is **best practice** to follow some guidelines in writing your mark up so your page is consistent, easy to read, easy to maintain, and professional-looking.

- Knowing the stricter XHTML rules can make you a better web designer with HTML5.

- Since HTML5 is not finished, no browsers on the market today will have full HTML5 support.

- You can check your browser's HTML5 compatibility by going to the http://html5test.com website.

- You can usually find the current version of your web browser by selecting "Help → About" or similar option from the web browser's menu.

- The doctype definition for HTML5 is simply "<!DOCTYPE html>".

- In HTML5, self-closing elements no longer require the self-closing slash (/).

- The small <**small**>, bold <**b**> and italic <**i**> elements have returned in HTML5.

- The <**a**> **name** attribute is now obsolete. You should use the **id** attribute instead.

- The <**a**> element can now wrap around multiple elements to link all of them to the same page.

- You no longer need the space and trailing slash at the end of the <**br**> element.

- You can use shorthand properties to string together values for several properties on one line.

Your Turn Activity: Using Updated HTML5 Elements

In this activity you are going to practice using the updated HTML5 elements on the Aquamaniacs home page. You will also create an initial "global.css" style sheet that will hold most of the site-wide styles.

Your activity requirements and instructions are found in the "Chapter_02_Activity.pdf" document located in your "KidCoder/AdvancedWebDesign/Activity Docs" folder. You can access this document through your Student Menu or by double-clicking on it from Windows Explorer or Mac OS Finder.

Complete this activity now and ensure you understand the material before continuing!

Chapter Three: Bringing Meaning to Markup

The HTML5 standard introduces new elements to help define different areas of a web page. In this chapter you are going to learn about "sections" that can be used to group related elements together.

Lesson One: Defining Areas with Sections

Web sites these days are no longer simple articles that follow one topic on each page. They have multiple columns, multiple topics and many chunks of possibly unrelated information. There might be navigation bars along the top and another set along the side. A main article might show up in the right column, but another article on a different topic is on the left. There could also be a side box with a calendar, a news section, and a list of books for sale. These complicated web pages might be easy to understand as a visual reader, but the HTML markup is very difficult to follow.

As a web designer you might mark each area of the page with a **<div>** element containing an "id" attribute.

```
<div id="myArea">
</div> <!-- end of myArea -->
```

With big areas it can be hard to visually match the ending **</div>** tag with the beginning **<div>** tag, so we can add comments to mark where each area ends. You can still follow this pattern, but HTML5 gives us some new elements to make things a little bit easier.

Layout vs. Meaning

Web pages are most often read by humans who understand the layout visually. If you arrange elements together on the page then we know they are probably related somehow in **meaning**. If you have a headline and then some content, the chances are those things belong together.

```
<div id="myArea">
  <h1>My 2 Dogs</h1>
  <img src="both_dogs.jpg"/>
</div> <!-- end of myArea -->
```

You can also apply CSS styles to these areas based on the "**id**" of the surrounding <**div**> element. We could make a fancier area in this example by centering our headline over the image with another color and font. So far there is nothing new here; we know how to do all of these things without HTML5.

However, today a web page is likely to be read by a **machine** as well as a human! A software program might scan a web page in order to read it to a blind person, or a search engine might read a page to find key words, or more advanced programs might try to understand the overall layout and major sections of the page. Because the <**div**> element is heavily used for **visual layouts**, it's not easy to also use <**div**> elements to identify the **meaning** of the content. Nested groups of <**div**> elements can get pretty complicated in order to let you style things the way you want visually. So it would be nice to wrap up everything in an area with a tidy element that clearly says everything inside is related in **meaning**.

Imagine a grocery store with different aisles for the bakery and meat department. When you walk in you can see the differences right away because all of the baked goods are in one place and the meat is arranged somewhere else. In order to make it super-obvious that there are two different departments, we could paint a big box on the floor around the bakery with a sign saying "BAKERY" and another box around the meat department with a sign saying "MEAT".

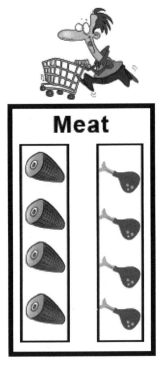

Customers can still find things in each area without reading the lines on the floor because they can see the chicken legs in one place and the donuts in the next aisle. However, now your helpful cleaning robot "Robbie" can be programmed to follow the lines on the floor to sweep the "BAKERY" and "MEAT" departments every night, and he doesn't have to look at the items on the shelf to figure out where he is within the store.

Introducing the HTML5 <section> Element

The HTML5 <section> element can be used to clearly group related elements together on a web page. The <section> is not a replacement for a <div>! <div> elements should continue to be used to apply styles and visually arrange things on a page. But a <section> can be added around groups of elements to show that they are related no matter how the page might visually appear to a human reader.

```
<section>
   Related elements can go in here and be visually arranged with <div> and styles
</section>
```

The <section> element may still need a **class** or **id** to describe what it contains. But the <section> itself at least says that everything inside forms a set of related items.

Using Headlines in Sections

In XHTML, you mostly used one or two main <h1> headline elements on your page. Perhaps there was one within the top header area and another to introduce your main content. This is still a fair practice, but the introduction of sections allows you to use more <h1> tags. HTML5 encourages you to add a <h1> element to the start of each <section>.

The <h1> says to the browser "the words inside this tag are the title of this area". That way each section has its own headline structure, kind of like a newspaper. A newspaper can have several unrelated articles on the front page, each with a title or headline describing the article content. If this standard is followed correctly, then sections can be picked up and moved around to other places or even other websites without needing much editing. Notice the section below contains a headline clearly describing the content.

```
<section>
   <h1>My 2 Dogs</h1>
   <img src="both_dogs.jpg"/>
</section>
```

<section> Elements are Rarely Used

As you have seen, a <section> element by itself defines a group of related elements. But think back to our grocery store example. Where are the big signs saying "BAKERY" or "MEAT"? A <section> does not have any identifying marks unless you add a **class** or **id** attribute, so it is a very general-purpose element that should only be used if nothing else works. HTML5 defines some more specialized elements for common kinds of sections like headers or footers. These elements are more often used on an HTML5 web page. You'll learn about them in the next lesson!

Lesson Two: Headers and Footers

The HTML5 authors looked at thousands of web sites and found that pages are often divided up in a similar way. They found header areas, navigation areas, articles to the left and right, and footers as well. So HTML5 has defined new elements to represent these common areas. In this lesson you'll learn about the new <**header**> and <**footer**> elements. These elements are more specialized kinds of sections, so you would use them instead of a general-purpose <**section**> element when you can.

The <header> Element

Many sites have some sort of banner or top area on each page. The new <**header**> element is used to hold this content. In XHTML you might use a <div id="header"> to mark and style this section, but in HTML5 you can just use a <**header**> instead.

XHTML	<div id="header"></div><!-- end of header-->
HTML5	<header></header>

The Footer Element

Another new HTML element is the <**footer**> element, which holds the footer information usually found on most web pages. HTML5 allows you to have multiple footer elements on a single page, but most often you'll just have one <**footer**> that replaces an earlier "<div id="footer">". A <**footer**> does not have to appear at the bottom of the page – but that is where you would most likely use it. The footer contains things like the copyright, related links, author information and other small print at the end of the page.

XHTML	<div id="footer"></div><!-- end of footer -->
HTML5	< footer></footer>

Work with Me: Using Header and Footer on the Home Page

You have already created an Aquamaniacs home page ("index.html") with old-style <**div**> elements for the header and footer. It's time to change those sections to use the new HTML5 elements.

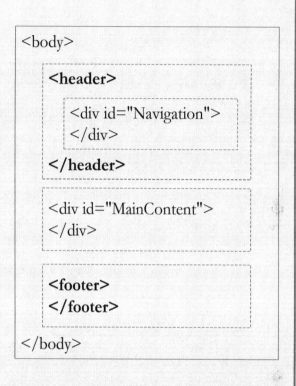

Open your Aquamaniacs "index.html" file in Komodo Edit or your text editor and make the following changes:

1. Replace the "<div id="Header">" element with a HTML5 <**header**> (and don't forget to change the closing tag as well). Also, type in the full header text, including a new tagline <**dive**> and <**h1**> as shown below.

```
<div id="Header">
<header>
    <div id="tagline">Creatures that Live Around and Under the Ocean
are ...</div>
    <h1>Aquamaniacs</h1>

    <div id="Navigation">
    </div>

</header>
</div>
```

2. Replace the "<div id="Footer">" element with an HTML5 **<footer>**, and don't forget to change the closing tag as well. Also, add in some footer copyright text as shown below.

```
<div id="Footer">
<footer>
    &copy;2013. Homeschool Programming. All Rights Reserved.
</footer>
</div>
```

3. Save your file and check the results in your web browser. You should see the new header and footer text appear.

Creatures that Live Around and Under the Ocean are ...

Aquamaniacs

Welcome to Aquamaniacs

Our oceans hold many wild and wonderful sea creatures. Here, you can learn about large animals like whales, dolphins, and sharks. See oddities like the sea urchin, longhorn cowfish, emperor penguin, lobster, lionfish, cuttlefish, and seahorse. Don't forget to visit the octopus and otter!

Follow our navigation links to learn about *"Big Critters"*. Check out the crazy things hidden under the *"Oddballs"* category. Enter our "Multimedia" lab for photos, sounds, and videos. Don't forget to see our *"Animation"* area for some funny effects!

©2013. Homeschool Programming. All Rights Reserved.

We'll apply some styles to the **<header>** and **<footer>** sections a little later.

If your web pages also used **<section>** elements, it's possible you could add a **<header>** and a **<footer>** within each **<section>**. But our Aquamaniacs project will not need more than one **<header>** at the top and one **<footer>** at the bottom of each page.

Lesson Three: Articles, Asides, and Navs

The <**header**> and <**footer**> aren't the only new HTML5 elements that describe areas of your web page. You can also identify areas using the <**article**>, <**aside**>, <**nav**> elements.

The <article> Element

You've seen newspapers that have several articles on the same page. Each article has a headline, author, and other content that is self-contained. That means the article by itself would make sense without the rest of the page. You could move the article to a different page or read it by itself. Similarly, a report, journal entry, presentation, or blog entry could each make sense by itself as long as each had a headline and other information. HTML5 uses the <**article**> element to hold content that is a self-contained article, especially when you have more than one article on the same page.

Before HTML5 you might have enclosed each article in a <**div**> with a shared **class** name so you could style all articles on the page. But with HTML5 you can just use <**article**> and apply styles to that element.

XHTML	<div class="article"></div><!-- end of article -->
HTML5	<article></article>

Remember, the same "class" can be used many times on a page to cover many elements. But an "id" can only be used once to identify a single element.

In this example, we've added two <**article**> elements to a page.

```
<article>
    <h1>Flying Disc Time!</h1>
    <cite>By Shadow</cite>
    <p>Calling all dogs!  Come out to the park tomorrow...</p>
</article>
<article>
    <h1>To Chase or Not to Chase?</h1>
    <cite>By Hunter</cite>
    <p>When you see a car driving by, do you immediately give chase?</p>
</article>
```

Within each <article> you can add other elements such as <h1>, <cite> to list the author or title, and so on. You can even add a <header> and <footer> to make very fancy articles!

As you can see to the right, the default <article> is a plain block element without any styling. But you can then apply any CSS styles you like to the <article> element.

Flying Disc Time!

By Shadow

Calling all dogs! Come out to the park tomorrow ...

To Chase or Not to Chase?

By Hunter

When you see a car driving by, do you immediately give chase?

The <nav> Element

In XHTML, you might create a <div> tag called "navigation" to set apart your main navigation area. But HTML5 has created a <nav> element that you can use instead to hold major navigation links. In most cases you'll use just one <nav> section near the top of your page to let readers move between the pages in your site.

XHTML	<div id="navigation"></div><!-- end of navigation -->
HTML5	< nav></nav>

A typical <nav> element might contain a list of hyperlinks like this:

```
<nav>
    <ul>
        <li><a href="hunter.html">View Hunter's Page</a></li>
        <li><a href="shadow.html">View Shadow's Page</a></li>
    </ul>
</nav>
```

Without any styling, these elements will just look like a flat list. But as you'll see later, we can apply styles to make this list look very different.

- View Hunter's Page
- View Shadow's Page

Human readers will quickly learn to skip over the navigation bar near the top or side if they are not looking for links. But a machine reader that wants to translate the page to audio for a sight-impaired person would like to skip over that area as well instead of re-reading the list of links every time. If the navigation bar is a simple <div> then it's hard to tell apart from the rest of the content, but a <nav> is easy to identify.

Work with Me: The Aquamaniacs Navigation Bar

Your Aquamaniacs web site will have many pages by the time you are done. Right now you just have an empty **<div>** representing the navigation area. Let's update that **<div>** to use an HTML5 **<nav>** element and also add in the links to all other pages that will eventually be part of our website.

Open your Aquamaniacs "index.html" file in Komodo Edit and make the following changes:

1. Replace the "<div id="Navigation">" element with an HTML5 **<nav>** (and don't forget to change the closing tag as well).

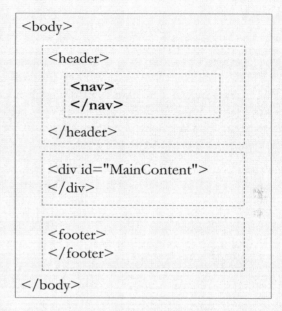

```
<div id="Navigation">
<nav>


</nav>
</div>
```

2. Next we want to add links to all the other pages in your site, even though they don't exist yet! It's easier to just do all of the links at one time. Because there are so many links, and you already know how to create lists of links, we have done the hard work for you. The contents for your **<nav>** bar can be found in the "Activity Starters/Chapter03/nav_element.txt" file.

    a. Open the "nav_element.txt" file in a text editor
    b. Select all of the text at once and copy it to the clipboard
    c. Switch over to your "index.html" file in Komodo Edit and place your text cursor on a blank line inside your **<nav>** element
    d. Paste the clipboard contents into that location

The code below shows the first part of your new **<nav>** element.

```
<nav>
    <ul>
        <!-- first link group -->
        <li id="home"><a href="index.html">Home</a>
        </li>
        <!-- second link group -->
        <li><a href="#">Big Critters</a>
            <ul>
                <li><a href="whales.html">Whales</a>
                <li><a href="dolphins.html">Dolphins</a>
                <li><a href="sharks.html">Sharks</a>
            </ul>
        </li>
    <!-- there are 5 total link groups; three are not shown here -->
</nav>
```

3. Save your "index.html" file and check the results in your web browser. You should see a list of hyperlinks below your header.

Creatures that Live Around and Under the Ocean are …

Aquamaniacs

- Home
- Big Critters
    - Whales
    - Dolphins
    - Sharks
- Oddballs

The 5 top-level headings are "Home", "Big Critters", "Oddballs", "Multimedia", and "Animation". Clicking on these top-level links will not do anything – they are just category headings.

All of the links under each heading like "Whales", "Dolphins", and "Sharks" will eventually lead to pages on your site. But we haven't created any of these pages yet, so if you try clicking on those links you'll just get a "File not Found" error.

4. Since the navigation bar takes up a lot of space right now, let's use our positioning skills to move it to the left side and push the "MainContent" **<div>** to the right. Open your "SiteStyle/global.css" style sheet and add the following three rules to the bottom:

```
nav {
    float: left;
    width: 20%;
}
```

```
#MainContent {
    float: right;
    width: 70%;
    margin-left: 10px;
}

footer {
    clear: both;
    text-align:center;
}
```

5. Save and check your work. You should now see the **<nav>** element float to the left and the "MainContent" **<div>** float to the right. The **<footer>** should be centered at the bottom.

Creatures that Live Around and Under the Ocean are ...

Aquamaniacs

- Home
- Big Critters
  - Whales
  - Dolphins
  - Sharks
- Oddballs
  - Emperor Penguin
  - Lobster
  - Lionfish
  - Cuttlefish
  - Seahorse
- Multimedia
  - Groovy Fish
  - Watery Pics
  - Aquarium
  - Sound Bites
  - Octopus Video
- Animation
  - Octopus Animation
  - Otters
  - Funny Fish 1
  - Funny Fish 2

Welcome to Aquamaniacs

Our oceans hold many wild and wonderful sea creatures. Here, you can learn about large animals like whales, dolphins, and sharks. See oddities like the sea urchin, longhorn cowfish, emperor penguin, lobster, lionfish, cuttlefish, and seahorse. Don't forget to visit the octopus and otter!

Follow our navigation links to learn about *"Big Critters"*. Check out the crazy things hidden under the *"Oddballs"* category. Enter our "Multimedia" lab for photos, sounds, and videos. Don't forget to see our *"Animation"* area for some funny effects!

©2013. Homeschool Programming. All Rights Reserved.

Later on you'll learn how to create a fancy navigation bar across the top with drop-down menus.

The <aside> Element

The <aside> element sets apart a section of content that is somewhat related to the main content, but could be removed without affecting the main information on the page. The best practice is to make sure the <aside> never includes content that should be in the main information area.

The <aside> element is not really defined by its position on the page, but it is often found on the side. You can use "<div class="sidebar">" to also define a small visual area. However, that <div> doesn't really describe the area as a related part of some larger concept. This is another example of using new HTML5 elements to add extra meaning to your layout even though the visual appearance might be the same.

XHTML	<div class="sidebar"></div><!-- end of sidebar -->
HTML5	< aside></aside>

Let's look at this example that contains an <article> and an <aside> within the article.

```
<article>
    <h1>Abandoned Pets</h1>
    <aside>Visit the <a href="http://www.humanesociety.org">Humane Society</a>
to learn how to help.</aside>
    <p>What happens to some pets when owners move away or get tired of them?</p>
</article>
```

The main article is about abandoned pets, and the <aside> gives the reader some extra information about helping out – but the article itself would still make sense even without the <aside>.

Now without any styling the <aside> element won't do much. But we can easily apply some style rules to the element to make it float off to the side with some smaller text:

```
aside{
    margin: 0 0 15px 25px;
    float: right;
    width: 150px;
    padding: 15px;
    font-size:
smaller;
}
```

Abandoned Pets

What happens to some pets when owners move away or get tired of them?

Visit the Humane Society to learn how to help.

In the next "Work with Me" section you are going to set up a second page in your Aquamaniacs site. This page will hold information about Dolphins.

 **Work with Me: Adding the Dolphins Page**

Let's add a new page to our website so we can experiment with the **<article>** and **<aside>** elements. We have created a "dolphins.html" page that you will add to your Aquamaniacs website. Then you will add some elements to the page and prepare it for styling in a later activity.

1. First, using Windows Explorer or Mac OS Finder, copy the "dolphins.html" file from your "KidCoder/AdvancedWebDesign/Activity Starters/Chapter03" directory to your "My Projects/Aquamaniacs" folder.

2. Next, in your Komodo Edit software, open the Aquamaniacs project and look at your projects panel on the left. If "dolphins.html" is not visible, right-click within that panel and select "Refresh View".

3. Now load "dolphins.html" in your web browser and confirm that you see default content similar to this:

Dolphins

Smart, Strong and Fast

Dolphins are a small marine mammal closely related to porpoises and whales. They live in the ocean, mostly in shallower areas and continental shelves and feed on fish and squid. Considered to be very intelligent, dolphins have a playful attitude and a friendly face which has made them very popular with people. Many aquariums have dolphin shows that show off how strong, smart, fast, and agile these incredible creatures are. These skills are also demonstrated if you have ever seen a dolphin in the wild riding the wake of your boat. The Ancient Greeks believed it was good luck to share your boat wake with a dolphin.

For More Information Visit: <u>Save the Dolphins</u>

Dolphin Dangers

You may think great big sharks and killer whales were the biggest threat to dolphins, but that is not true. Yes, they are eaten for lunch on a regular basis but humans are actually the biggest threat to

The "MainContent" area has a **<h1>**, **<h2>**, and **<p>** at the top. Underneath it also has an additional paragraph, hyperlink, and third paragraph.

We want to arrange this Dolphins page so the bottom content is wrapped within an **<article>**. The hyperlink will go into an **<aside>** element to the right-hand side.

When you are done you won't see much visual change, but our page will be ready for styling in the next activity!

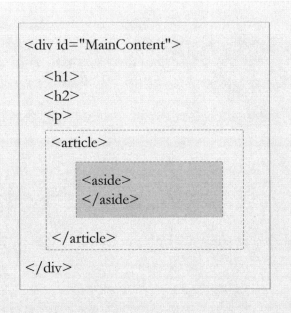

4. Add an **<article>** tag around the last two paragraphs and headline

```
<article>
   <p>For More Information Visit: <a href="http://www.bluevoice.org/">Save
the Dolphins</a></p>
   <h1>Dolphin Dangers</h1>
   <p>You may think great big sharks and killer whales. . .</p>
</article>
```

5. Next, add an **<aside>** element around the top paragraph in the second article.

```
<article>
   <aside>
     <p>For More Information Visit: <a href="http://www.bluevoice.org/">Save
the Dolphins</a></p>
   </aside>
   <h1>Dolphin Dangers</h1>
```

6. When you are done, save your file and re-load it in your web browser. The headlines may be a bit smaller, but otherwise you won't notice much difference yet.

Chapter Review

- HTML5 contains new elements to make dividing a web page into meaningful areas much easier.

- Today a web page is likely to be read by a **machine** as well as a human.

- Because the **<div>** element is heavily used for **visual layouts**, it's not easy to also use **<div>** elements to identify the **meaning** of the content.

- The HTML5 **<section>** element can be used to clearly group related elements together on a web page – although it is not a replacement for the **<div>** element!

- HTML5 encourages you to add a **<h1>** element to the start of each **<section>**.

- The **<section>** element itself is actually rarely used – instead HTML5 defines more specialized elements for handling different kinds of content.

- The **<header>** and **<footer>** elements allow you to create top banners and bottom small print.

- HTML5 uses the **<article>** element.to hold content that is a self-contained article. Article content makes sense even without the rest of the page.

- The **<nav>** element can be used to hold major navigation links.

- The **<aside>** element sets apart a section of content that is somewhat related to the main content but could be removed without affecting the main information on the page.

Your Turn Activity: Styling Articles and Asides

Your Dolphins web page has two articles and an aside, but they don't look very interesting. In this activity you are going to apply a variety of styles to the article and aside elements to get a more professional look.

Your activity requirements and instructions are found in the "Chapter_03_Activity.pdf" document located in your "KidCoder/AdvancedWebDesign/Activity Docs" folder. You can access this document through your Student Menu or by double-clicking on it from Windows Explorer or Mac OS Finder.

Complete this activity now and ensure you understand the material before continuing!

Chapter Four: Figures and Annotations

You already know how to add simple images to your web page. HTML5 introduces a few new elements and style options to let you more easily group together images with captions and annotations (or notes).

Lesson One: Figures and Captions

In this lesson, we'll take a look at some changes to the way you can handle images in HTML5. Remember that an image can be placed on your page with the **<img>** element. This same element works in HTML5.

XHTML	**<img src=**"file" **alt=**"A description" **width=**"xx" **height=**"yy"**/>**
HTML5	**<img src=**"file" **alt=**"A description" **width=**"xx" **height=**"yy"**>**

The only difference is that you don't need to use the self-closing slash "/>" to end the element. HTML5 allows you to end the element with a single angle bracket ">". The **src** attribute continues to hold a relative or absolute path to your image file. The **alt** attribute should contain a text description of your image. Of course, the **width** and **height** attributes control the size of the image on the page.

The <figure> Element

You can add a caption to an image using a **<div>** and paragraph **<p>** elements with some styling. However, HTML5 defines some new elements to make image captioning easier and more obvious. To start, the **<figure>** element can be used as an outer wrapper to neatly contain an image and a caption.

```
<figure>
    <img src="octopus.png" alt="My crazy octopus" width="380" height="250">
</figure>
```

By itself the **<figure>** wrapper doesn't make much visual difference. But by using this tag you make it easier to style your figures later. You can also add a caption (a small text description) to the **<figure>** as we'll show you next.

The <figcaption> Element

The <**figcaption**> element works directly with the <**figure**> element to add a caption to all content appearing inside the figure. While a <**figcaption**> obviously belongs to the parent <**figure**>, you will still want to apply CSS styles to your <**figcaption**> to control the way it looks on your page.

```
<figure>
    <img src="octopus.png" alt="My crazy octopus" width="380" height="250">
    <figcaption>A loveable pet!</figcaption>
</figure>
```

In the example above, the caption is placed under the image. You can also move the <**figcaption**> element above the <**img**> to show the caption above the image.

Note that you can also place headlines, paragraphs, or other content within your figure. Just make sure that content is directly related to your image.

A loveable pet!

Work with Me: Watery Pictures

You are now going to create several figures and captions on a new page called "creatures.html".

1. Using Windows Explorer or Mac OS Finder, copy "creatures.html" from your "Activity Starters/Chapter04" folder to "MyProjects/Aquamaniacs".
2. Also using Explorer or Finder, create a folder called "PagePhotos" underneath your "MyProjects/Aquamaniacs" folder.
3. Using Explorer or Finder, copy the following images from "Activity Starters/Chapter04/PagePhotos" to your new "Aquamaniacs/PagePhotos" folder:
   - "tufted-puffin.jpg"
   - "plumose-anemone.jpg"
   - "wolfeel.jpg"

4. Load your "creatures.html" file in a web browser to confirm it looks like the screen shown to the right. The page should show three pictures, each with its own headline.

5. Run Komodo Edit, open the "creatures.html" file, and find the "MainContent" area shown below.

Water Creatures

A Tufted Puffin

A Plumose Anemone

A Wolf Eel

```
<div id="MainContent">


    <h1>Water Creatures</h1>


    <h2>A Tufted Puffin</h2>
    <img src="PagePhotos/tufted-puffin.jpg"
     alt="A tufted puffin." width="300" height="338">


    <h2>A Plumose Anemone</h2>
    <img src="PagePhotos/plumose-anemone.jpg"
     alt="A plumose anemone." width="300" height="331">


    <h2>A Wolf Eel</h2>
    <img src="PagePhotos/wolfeel.jpg"
     alt="A wolf eel." width="300" height="276">


</div><!-- end of MainContent -->
```

6. Now, add **<figure>** and **<figcaption>** elements around each of the three groups of headlines and images. Use your imagination to come up with the best captions!

Here is an example for the first picture:

```
<figure>
    <h2>A Tufted Puffin</h2>
    <img src="PagePhotos/tufted-puffin.jpg" alt="A tufted puffin."
        width="300" height="338">
    <figcaption>This is my happy face.</figcaption>
</figure>
```

7. Repeat the addition of **<figure>** and **<figcaption>** elements for the other two pictures.

8. When you are done, reload your "creatures.html" page in your web browser and confirm that each picture now has a caption.

Water Creatures

A Tufted Puffin

This is my happy face.

A Plumose Anemone

Which way is up?

A Wolf Eel

Welcome to the pack.

Lesson Two: Figure Annotation with Relative Positioning

An **annotation** is a small note you can add to a picture. If you've ever "tagged" someone in Facebook, you have seen annotations in the form of boxes drawn around the faces of the people in your pictures. Annotations can be made up of simple text or fancier graphics.

In this example, we have added three annotations to our octopus: "Googly Eyes", "Cheezy Smile", and "Tentacle".

These effects are pretty easy to create with HTML5 and CSS using these steps:

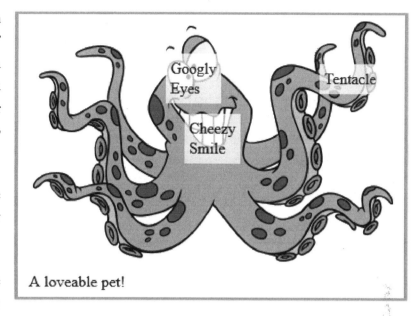

1. Use a special class of **<figure>** and an unordered list **<ul>** within the **<figcaption>** element. Each list item **<li>** contains one annotation.
2. Apply inline styles to each **<li>** with specific location information
3. Add style rules to your CSS to control the positioning and other special effects

Creating Annotations in a List

To create a nice annotation on an image, your first step is to ensure that you are using the HTML5 **<figure>** and **<figcaption>** elements. Add a **class** attribute to your **<figure>** element so we can easily create style rules applying to any annotated figure. We have chosen the class name "**annotated**", but you can use any name you like. Then within your **<figcaption>**, add an unordered list **<ul>** with some list items **<li>** containing each annotation or piece of text you want to show in the image.

```
<figure class="annotated">
    <img src="octopus.png" alt="My crazy octopus" width="380" height="250">
    <figcaption>A loveable pet!
      <ul>
        <li>Googly Eyes</li>
        <li>Cheezy Smile</li>
        <li>Tentacle</li>
      </ul>
    </figcaption>
</figure>
```

So far this extra list will just appear underneath the caption. But we really want to move each list item to a specific location on the image.

Inline Location Styles for List Items

In order to place each list item on the image in the right location, we need to know the coordinates for each spot. A **coordinate** is a pair of values that counts the number of pixels over and down from the top-left corner of the image.

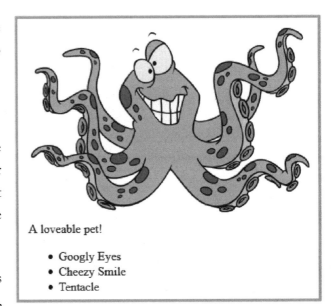

A loveable pet!

- Googly Eyes
- Cheezy Smile
- Tentacle

The top-left corner of an image is written as coordinate (0,0). As you move pixels to the right, the first value increases, so (10,0) would be a pixel 10 places over from the left side. Similarly, as you move down the image, the second value increases. The coordinates (10,20) would point to a spot 10 pixels to the right and 20 pixels down from the top-left corner.

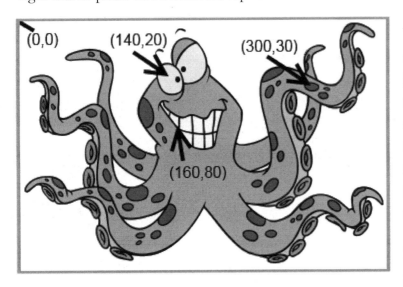

You can figure out coordinates for any spot on an image using an image editor. Usually just hovering your mouse over a spot will show the coordinates somewhere on the screen. Or you can just guess with some trial and error until you home in on the right spot. The image to the left shows the key locations for each annotation, plus the top-left (0,0) coordinate for reference.

Now that we know the locations for each piece of text, we want to set those locations using the CSS properties **left** and **top**. The **left** property will hold the number of pixels across from the left side, and the **top** property will hold the number of pixels down from the top edge. Because each list item will have different coordinates, we will apply these properties inline directly on each element instead of using a separate CSS file.

```
<ul>
    <li style="left: 140px; top:20px;">Googly Eyes</li>
    <li style="left: 160px; top:80px">Cheezy Smile</li>
    <li style="left: 300px; top:30px">Tentacle</li>
</ul>
```

Unfortunately just adding these top and left coordinates with styles is not enough; you won't see any visible change in our image! Location of elements on the screen can be done using *absolute* or *relative* positioning. We covered the **position** property in detail in our first-semester course, so you may want to look back on that material for a reminder.

In order to place the annotations in the right spots, we need to add three CSS rules. First, we want to add a rule for the "annotated" class that changes the **position** to *relative*. This style tells the browser that elements inside may be positioned somewhere other than their default positions.

```
.annotated
{
    position:relative;
}
```

Next we need to add a style rule for the unordered list <**ul**> inside the annotated figure. These properties should all be familiar to you from earlier work. We are removing the bullet icons from the list and setting the font size. The absolute position is very important, because it tells the browser to place the <**ul**> element exactly at the top and left positions shown (0,0) relative to the parent <**figure**>.

```
.annotated ul{
    list-style:none;
    position:absolute;
    top:0;
    left:0;
    font-size:16px;
}
```

Now we can start seeing some results in our browser! The list items appear near the top-left corner of the figure. We have successfully positioned the entire list element <**ul**>, but the individual locations for each <**li**> are still being ignored. We will need to add a third style rule to make those take effect.

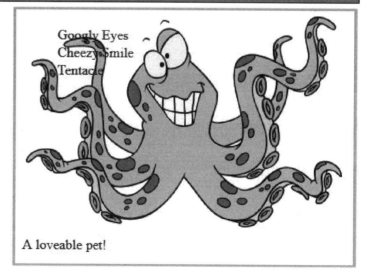

A loveable pet!

The style rule below will change the behavior of the individual list items <li> in our annotated figure. Most importantly, we change the positioning to absolute, which will allow the top and left properties we set on each element to take effect. Those elements will now be positioned according to the pixel coordinates from the top-left corner of the parent figure. In addition, we add a **width**, **height**, some **padding** and a **background-color** to make the annotations stand out from the image.

```
.annotated li{
    position:absolute;
    width: 50px;
    height: 40px;
    padding: 5px;
    background-color:rgba(255,255,255,0.8);
}
```

The format of the **background-color** property one you have not seen before. You know that colors can be set using Red, Green, and Blue components (RGB), and each component is a value between 0 and 255. You can set those values using normal decimal numbers or hexadecimal numbers #00 - #FF. So why do we have a fourth value "0.8" at the end?

This fourth value is called the **alpha** or **transparency** value. The alpha value should be between 0.0 and 1.0. A value of 0.0 means the color is completely transparent and won't be seen at all. A value of 1.0 means the color is completely solid and won't let anything underneath show through. Any value in between such as 0.2, 0.5, or 0.8 will block 20%, 50%, or 80% of the underlying image.

Now we can see good results from our hard work. Each list item is positioned on top of the image with correct locations, and the text has a nice background that makes it readable but still shows some of the underlying image.

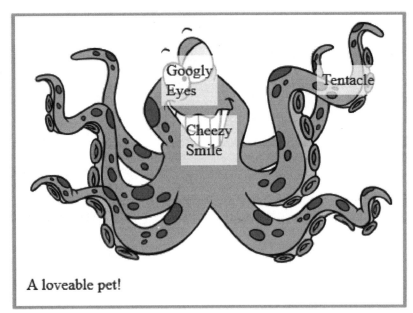

A loveable pet!

In the next lesson you will learn how to make annotations appear only when the user hovers a mouse on top of them. But first, it's time to put your new knowledge to work on the Aquamaniacs website.

Work with Me: Aquarium Annotations

In this activity you are going to add a new "Aquarium" page to your Aquamaniacs website. The aquarium will have an annotated image of fish swimming in the fish tank.

1. To begin, use Windows Explorer or Mac OS Finder to copy the "aquarium.html" file from your "Activity Starters/Chapter04" folder to your "MyProjects/Aquamaniacs" directory. Also copy the "aquarium.jpg" file from "Activity Starters/Chapter04/PagePhotos" to your "MyProjects/Aquamaniacs/PagePhotos" directory.

2. Load the "aquarium.html" file from your Aquamaniacs folder into your web browser and make sure you can see the picture and list of annotations underneath the caption.

   You will not have to make any changes to "aquarium.html" for this activity. All of your work will be inside the "global.css" file.

Aquarium Tank

Spotting Seven Fish

A group of fish swimming in an aquarium.

- Fish 1
- Fish 2
- Fish 3
- Fish 4
- Fish 5
- Fish 6
- Fish 7

3. Now, load your "Aquamaniacs/SiteStyle/global.css" file in your Komodo Edit software. Scroll down to the bottom of the page, and add the three styles for "annotated" figures, lists, and list items exactly as described in the lesson.

```css
.annotated {
    position:relative;
}
.annotated ul{
    list-style:none;
    position:absolute;
    top:0;
    left:0;
    font-size:16px;
}
.annotated li{
    position:absolute;
    width: 50px;
    height: 40px;
    padding: 5px;
    background-color:rgba(255,255,255,0.8);
}
```

4. Save your changes and reload "aquarium.html" in your web browser. You should now see the "Fish1" through "Fish7" annotations appear in different places on the image.

In the next lesson you'll learn how to apply some other special effects to your figure annotations.

Spotting Seven Fish

A group of fish swimming in an aquarium.

Lesson Three: Dynamic Annotations

We can use some style properties to make annotations appear only when the user's mouse is hovering over the image or the list item. That way the annotations don't block the underlying image all the time.

The "text-indent" Property

The **text-indent** property controls the spacing for the first line in a block of text. It can be applied to paragraphs to add an indentation on the first line of each paragraph.

```
<p style="text-indent:10px;">This is my indented paragraph.</p>
<p>This paragraph has no indentation.</p>
```

Positive numbers like "10px" move the text that many pixels to the right. But negative numbers will move the text to the left, and this feature is often used as a styling trick to hide text completely!

> **This is my indented paragraph.**
>
> **This paragraph has no indentation.**

```
<p style="text-indent:-9999px;">This is my indented paragraph.</p>
<p>This paragraph has no indentation.</p>
```

In this example, we have used a very large negative value (-9999) that will move the text so far to the left you can't see it at all!

> **This paragraph has no indentation.**

The ":hover" State

How can we use this feature? Remember how we used the ":hover" state to style anchor links <**a**> when the user's mouse was hovering over the link? In HTML5 and CSS3 we can do the same thing for other elements! We can set the **text-indent** property to one value to hide the element when the mouse is away, and set the **text-indent** to another value to show the element when the mouse is hovering over it. Instead of paragraphs <**p**>, we are going to style the list items <**li**> for the annotated class.

```
.annotated li{
    position:absolute;
    width: 50px;
    height: 40px;
    padding: 5px;
    background-color:rgba(255,255,255,0.8);
    text-indent: -9999px;
}
```

Here we have removed the background color for the list item and set a large negative text-indent. That way, the basic figure will not show any text or background boxes at all, just the plain image.

Now we can add a new style rule with the ":hover" state attached to the "annotated" class. This means the style rule will only apply whenever the mouse is hovering over any part of the "annotated" elements.

```
.annotated:hover li
{
    border:2px solid black;
    background-color:rgba(255,255,255,0.8);
    text-indent: 0px;
}
```

The style adds a thin black border, a partially transparent background, and resets the **text-indent** to 0. That way, when the mouse cursor is hovering over any part of the octopus, we'll see all of our annotations in a nicely framed box.

We can make our style rules even more specific to only show the text in a box when the mouse is hovering over that text item. Take a careful look at the selectors ".annotated:hover li" and ".annotated li:hover" below.

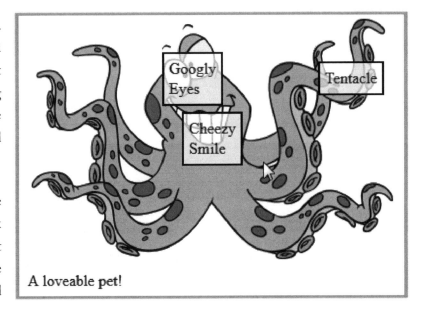

A loveable pet!

```
.annotated:hover li
{
    border:2px solid black;
    background-color:rgba(255,255,255,0.8);
    text-indent: 0px;
}
.annotated li:hover
{
    background-color: white;
    text-indent: 0px;
}
```

The first selector will be active whenever the mouse is hovering over any element in the "annotated" class. The annotation text will still be hidden and a semi-transparent box will show in each list item location. The second selector will be active when the mouse is hovering over a **<li>** element in the "annotated class". In that case the annotation underneath the mouse will have a solid white background and visible text.

Let's see these styles in action! The bottom left image shows the first style with the mouse cursor hovering over the octopus outside of the list item boxes. The bottom right image shows the second style taking effect when the mouse cursor is hovering over one of the boxes.

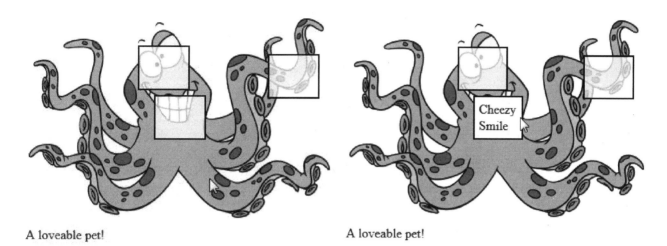

A loveable pet!   A loveable pet!

The "cursor" Property

Using the "hover" state on elements other than hyperlinks is a new feature in CSS3. Some browsers may change the mouse cursor to a crosshair (+) or text pointer (I) when you are hovering over elements, and this is confusing to users.

We want to make sure that the mouse cursor behaves exactly the way we want it to, so we will add a **cursor** property to our annotated list items. We used the **cursor** property to style anchor links <a> in our first semester course, but now we will use it to control the annotations as well. We can use the *default* value to get the standard arrow ( ).

```
.annotated li:hover
{
    background-color: white;
    text-indent: 0px;
    cursor: default;
}
```

Now when we hover over an annotation list item, the mouse cursor will not change in unexpected ways. The exact appearance of each cursor depends on your operating system.

Work with Me: Dynamic Fish Annotations

Let's return to our new "Aquarium" page showing fish in a tank. Right now the annotations are fixed in place, so let's use our new **text-indent**, **cursor**, and **:hover** styles to improve the behavior.

1. Run Komodo Edit and load your "global.css" file. Scroll down to the bottom and make the same modifications to your annotated list items that we described in the lesson above.

2. First, modify the existing ".annotated li" rule to remove the **background-color** and add a **text-indent**. That way the annotations will be completely hidden when the mouse is somewhere else.

```
.annotated li{
    position:absolute;
    width: 50px;
    height: 40px;
    padding: 5px;
    background-color:rgba(255,255,255,0.8);
    text-indent: -9999px;
}
```

3. Then, add a ":hover" rule for the entire annotated figure that will make the background boxes appear when the mouse is hovering over the whole figure.

```
.annotated:hover li
{
    border:2px solid black;
    background-color:rgba(255,255,255,0.8);
}
```

4. Finally, add a ":hover" rule for the individual annotated list items to make the text appear on a solid white background when the mouse is hovering over the box.

```
.annotated li:hover
{

    background-color: white;
    text-indent: 0px;
    cursor: default;

}
```

5. Save your changes to "global.css" and reload "aquarium.html" in your web browser. Does it behave the way you expect? You should see no annotations or background boxes when the mouse is off the **\<figure\>** area entirely.

Moving the mouse cursor anywhere within the **<figure>** element should make the annotation background boxes appear.

Finally, hovering the mouse over one of the boxes will make that annotation text visible.

 ## Chapter Review

- The <**img**> element no longer requires the self-closing slash "/" to end the element.

- The <**figure**> element can be used as an outer wrapper to neatly contain an image.

- The <**figcaption**> element works directly with the <**figure**> element to add an image caption.

- You can apply styles to the <**figure**> and <**figcaption**> elements separately.

- You can also place headlines, paragraphs, or other content within your <**figure**>.

- An **annotation** is a small note you can add to a picture.

- A **coordinate** value pair counts the number of pixels over and down from the image top-left corner.

- The top-left corner of an image is written as coordinate (0,0). The first value increases as you move to the right and the second value increases as you move down the screen.

- The CSS properties **left** and **top** can be used to position an element on the screen.

- *Relative* positioning says that elements may appear somewhere other than their default locations.

- The **background-color** property can take up to four parameters: 3 values for colors (red, green and blue) and one value for the alpha or transparency value.

- The alpha or transparency value sets how transparent the color will appear on the screen. A value of 1.0 is completely solid and a value of 0.0 is completely see-through.

- The **text-indent** property controls the spacing for the first line in a block of text.

- Negative numbers in the **text-indent** property will move the text to the left on the screen. Setting the value to a large negative number will make the text disappear on the screen.

- The **cursor** property will change the look of the mouse pointer on the screen.

Your Turn Activity: Leaping Dolphins

In this activity you are going to add some site-wide styles to your figures and captions, and then test them out with a new figure on the "Dolphins" page. You'll also add some styling to the <**footer**> to improve the overall look of your pages.

Your activity requirements and instructions are found in the "Chapter_04_Activity.pdf" document located in your "KidCoder/AdvancedWebDesign/Activity Docs" folder. You can access this document through your Student Menu or by double-clicking on it from Windows Explorer or Mac OS Finder.

Complete this activity now and ensure you understand the material before continuing!

Chapter Five: Adding Audio and Video

Web pages can contain audio (sound) and video (movie) clips as well as text and images. In this chapter, you will learn several ways to add audio and video to your web pages.

Lesson One: Linked and Embedded Videos

Web browsers all have the built-in ability to display text and pictures. But showing a video is a bit more complicated. Over time a number of different video file formats have been created, and each of the major web browsers and operating systems has different levels of support for each format.

Video File Types

The table below describes some of the major video file formats you may find online.

File Type	Description
.AVI or .WMV	**Windows Media Video** Microsoft formats will play on Windows computers.
.MPEG or .MP4	The popular **Moving Pictures Expert Group** formats can be played on many different operating systems and on most major browsers.
.MOV	The **QuickTime** format was developed by Apple and can be played on any computer that has installed the free QuickTime player.
.WEBM	The **WebM** format developed by Google is designed to be a free, open-source format that works well with new HTML5 video elements.
.SWF or .FLV	**Flash** videos were developed by Macromedia (now Adobe). Browsers used to come pre-installed with Flash players, but newer HTML5 technologies are starting to replace Flash. Apple iOS products (phone and tablets) do not have Flash support.
.OGG or .OGV	These free, high-quality container formats have no patent or licensing restrictions. .OGG is used mostly for audio files and .OGV for video.

Some browsers need special plug-in pieces of software to play certain video types (such as Flash). Other video formats can be played directly by a web browser, or are not supported at all. Newer web browsers may add or remove support for certain video types, so it's hard to find one type that will work everywhere.

Before HTML5 was created, you had a few ways to add video files to your web page:

- Directly linked videos
- Embedded YouTube™ videos
- Embedded Flash™ videos

All of these approaches still work today, so let's explore each of them.

Directly Linked Videos

You can create an anchor <**a**> hyperlink to any file, including video files. The example below shows a link to a MP4 video.

```
<a href="hunter_shadow.mp4">Click here for a video of Hunter and Shadow</a>
```

Your video will not appear "embedded" within the web page, but it will appear as a plain text hyperlink. When you click on a hyperlink the web browser will figure out what to do with the video file.

<u>Click here for a video of Hunter and Shadow</u>

If you are using a standard, popular file format like MP4 then your browser is likely to play it without problems. But you have no control over where or how the video plays… it might be a full screen display, hiding the existing page. You are relying on your web browser to have already installed any plug-in players such as QuickTime or Flash Player that may be needed for that format. Web users can also choose to download any hyperlinked file to their local computer.

Embedded YouTube Videos

One easy way to put videos on your web page is to let someone else host them on their computer systems, and just "embed" links to the video on your page. YouTube™ (www.YouTube.com) is a great example. The videos you see on YouTube can be embedded on your web page with a few simple steps.

When viewing your target video on YouTube, click on the "Share" tab and then the "Embed" tab. In the box underneath, you will see some HTML code that can be directly copied into your web page.

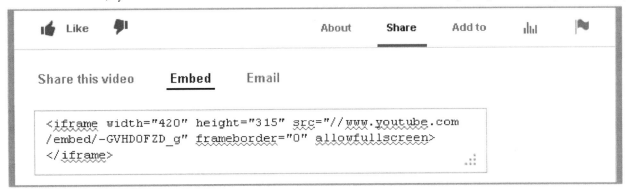

Copy the entire block of HTML code from the text box into your own HTML page where you want the video to appear.

```
<p>This video shows my 2 dogs Hunter and Shadow.</p>
<iframe width="420" height="315" src="http://www.youtube.com/embed/-GVHD0FZD_g"
frameborder="0" allowfullscreen></iframe>
```

Look closely at the **src** attribute you get from YouTube, and make sure it contains a valid URL. If it is missing an initial "http:" or other required part, you can fix that on your own.

When you load your page with embedded YouTube video, the video will appear directly within the page with Play, Volume, and other controls along the bottom. Just click the arrow button to play the video!

Embedded Flash Videos

For many years, the Adobe Flash format (.SWF or .FLV) was the king of Internet videos. Most browsers came with the Flash Player plug-in automatically, and you could download the free Flash plug-in from the Adobe website if needed. However, the Flash format is (over a long period of time) going to be replaced by newer formats and HTML5. Already, Apple devices based on iOS come without native Flash support. So we will show you how to embed Flash videos, but you don't need to install the Flash Player yourself.

To add a Flash movie to a web page, you can use either the <**embed**> element or the <**object**> element anywhere inside the <**body**>. The <**object**> element gives you some extra options, but it is very complicated, so we will skip the <**object**> approach. The HTML5 <**embed**> element is a general-purpose way to place content needing an extra plug-in (like Flash Player) to view.

```
<embed src="flash-file.swf" width="400" height="300">
```

The **src** attribute should contain the filename or URL of the video file. You can add the **width** and

height attributes to control the size of the object on the web page. Your web browser will then figure out what plug-in to use to display the file.

Of course you don't have much control over the appearance of the video, the buttons the player shows, and whether or not the movie starts playing right away.

Making or Finding Videos

You may remember from our first-semester course that finding images for your website can be a bit tricky. All images you find online are owned by someone, and you need to have permission to use those images. Videos, sounds, and other types of media are no different!

One way to make sure you have permission is to use your own video. Today, most smart-phones have built-in cameras that can make small video clips. Then you can download the video to your computer with a USB cable. Your phone may let you automatically share your movie to different social media websites. You can also make videos using a webcam hooked up to your computer. Of course not everyone has an easy way to create a new video, so you might find existing video clips online instead.

The Internet is full of free and downloadable video clips, so you can search for and download many different video files. You probably want to search for "MP4 clips" that are reasonably short, and avoid full-length movies that are large and have potential copyright issues. **Always use adult supervision when exploring new web sites!** If you find a movie online, make sure you carefully read and understand the copyright information before embedding that movie on your own page. YouTube, for example, has several helpful pages relating to copyright subjects.

Lesson Two: HTML5 Video

HTML5 is a new web standard, still in the finishing stages. But some useful elements have already been adopted by most major web browsers, including a new way to play video clips.

The HTML5 <video> and <source> Elements

The <**video**> element is a new, powerful way to show videos on your web page. This element will let you list several different file formats for the same video in order to handle differences in the major browsers.

Here is an example:

```
<video width="" height="300" preload="auto" controls>
    <source src="hunter_shadow.mp4" type="video/mp4"/>
    <source src="hunter_shadow.ogg" type="video/ogg"/>
    <source src="hunter_shadow.webm" type="video/webm"/>
  Your browser does not support the video tag.
</video>
```

The <**video**> element contains the **width** and **height** attributes, which are optional but recommended. If you set just one attribute, the web browser will figure out the other attribute based on the actual file. Here we have set the **height** to 300, meaning the video will be exactly 300 pixels high and however wide is necessary to display without stretching or shrinking.

Inside the <**video**> element you can place one or more <**source**> elements. Each <**source**> represents one video file format. The **src** attribute contains the filename or URL, and the **type** attribute contains a description of the type. The three main video file formats you can use with this tag are MP4 (type="video/mp4"), OGG (type="video/ogg"), and WEBM (type="video/webm").

Most browsers support all of these formats, but some browsers might only support one or two formats. Therefore, if you can create the same video file in different formats, you can add more than one <**source**> element as shown above. Browsers will search the list looking for a format they can safely play. If a browser can't understand the HTML5 <**video**> tag at all it will show the text underneath the <**source**> elements ("Your browser does not support the video tag").

Let's take a closer look at the attributes on the <video> element.

```
<video width="" height="300" preload="auto" controls>
```

There are several optional attributes such as **preload** and **controls** that control how the video will behave inside the browser. The table below describes the most common options:

<video> Attribute	Description
autoplay	If present, the video will start playing as soon as the page loads
controls	If present, the video frame will include common controls such as play or pause
loop	If present, the video will play in an endless loop
muted	If present, the video sound will be turned off
preload	Video files can be large, so this option lets you guide how the video file will be loaded. "*auto*" means load the entire video right away. "*metadata*" means load only information about the video, but not the video itself. "*none*" means don't load anything right away. When the user clicks on the video to play it, any missing information or files is then loaded.

The first four attributes can be added with their name only, and no value! This is a bit different than you have seen before. Just placing the name as an attribute is enough to control the behavior, as shown below.

```
<video autoplay controls loop muted>
```

The result on our web page is pretty nice! We can embed the video, control the size, and let the user pause and play using built-in buttons. It is best practice to avoid using **autoplay**, because users often don't want a video to start playing automatically as soon as the page loads. Let them click the play button instead.

Styling Videos

Now that HTML5 has a dedicated <video> element, it's easy to apply CSS rules to videos. In your style sheet, just use "video" as your selector to apply styles to all <video> elements.

```
video {
}
```

You might want to give your videos some margin and paddings, float styles, borders, or other special effects. You'll get a chance to add a video to your Aquamaniacs website and apply some styles in the next "Work with Me" section.

Work with Me: Octopus Videos

Let's use what you learned to add a video of an Octopus to your Aquamaniacs website. We have already created an HTML page "octopus-video.html" and have a video clip in a MP4 and OGV format. You will need to copy the video files and the starting HTML file into your project, add the <**video**> tags to the HTML page, and create some new styles in your "global.css".

1. To begin, using Windows Explorer or Mac OS Finder, create a new directory called "Media" in your "MyProjects/Aquamaniacs" folder. The "MyProjects/Aquamaniacs/Media" folder will hold all of our website's audio and video files, similar to the way "PagePhotos" holds the images.

2. Next, copy the "octopus-video.html" file from your "Activity Starters/Chapter05" directory to the "MyProjects/Aquamaniacs" folder.

3. Finally, copy the "octopus.mp4" and "octopus.ogv" files from "Activity Starters/Chapter05/Media" to your new "Aquamaniacs/Media" folder.

4. Load the "Aquamaniacs/octopus-video.html" file into your web browser and make sure you can see the initial text. The video is not there yet!

The Octopus

Master of Disguise

The octopus is found all around the world

Now, load the "octopus-video.html" file into Komodo Edit and place your cursor in between the second headline and the opening paragraph.

5. Add the <**video**> element as shown below.

```
<h2>Master of Disguise</h2>
<video width="352" height="288" preload controls>
   <source src="Media/octopus.ogv" type="video/ogg">
   <source src="Media/octopus.mp4" type="video/mp4">
   Your browser does not support the video tag.
</video>
<p>The octopus is found all around the world living in rocky holes
```

6. Save your file and check it in a browser. The octopus video should now appear in between the headline and the paragraph.

Master of Disguise

The octopus is found all around the world living in rocky holes

7. Next, open your "global.css" file and go down to the bottom. Add the following style rule for the video element.

```
video {
    float: left;
    margin: 0 15px 10px 0;
    padding: 10px;
    border:2px solid #CCCCCC;
    background-color: black;
}
```

This style should make the video float to the left with paragraph text wrapped around it to the right. We've also added some margins and padding and a thin gray border.

8. Save your changes to "global.css" and reload your "octopus-video.html" file in your web browser to see the results.

Master of Disguise

The octopus is found all around the world living in rocky holes under the ocean. It is a fascinating creature with eight legs, and each leg has hundreds of sucker pads. Even though it looks incredibly soft and weak, the octopus can take care of itself quite well. A master of disguise, this creature can use a network of pigment cells and special muscles in its skin to instantly match the colors, patterns and textures of any background it encounters. This ability to camouflage itself is so good, predators and prey may not even notice the octopus hanging out in front of them. If it is noticed, the octopus will squirt a cloud of black ink so the attacker can't see and its sense of smell is numbed. The fast swimming octopus can quickly jet away or squeeze its soft body into a small hole where the predator can't reach.

Lesson Three: HTML5 Audio

The history of audio (sound) support in web browsers is pretty similar to video. Early browsers could only play sounds using plug-in components for each sound file format. Many sound file formats were created over time, and not all browsers supported all formats. Fortunately, HTML5 has a new <audio> element that works just like the <video> tag and takes away much of the confusion.

Audio File Formats

There are many competing audio formats, and each has different strengths and weaknesses. Some formats are good at compressing sound to very small file sizes, but you might hear poorer quality sound. Other formats have a free, open-source standard that does not require any expensive software to create or play.

File Type	Description
.AIFF	The **Audio Interchange File Format** by Apple contains high quality (uncompressed) sound but has a large file size
.MP3	The **MPEG Layer III Audio** by the Moving Picture Experts Group (MPEG) group compresses audio to a small size.
.OGG	The **OGG** format was developed as a free open source audio container
.WAV	**Waveform Audio Files** hold high quality (uncompressed) sound with a large file size
.WMA	**Windows Media Audio** files on Windows include copy protection features

Today MP3 is a very popular format, but the software to play it is not free. Open source browsers are not as likely to support MP3 files because the music is not in a free, open format.

The HTML5 <audio> Element

The new HTML5 <audio> element lets you embed sound clips directly into your web page. This element works in all the modern browsers and is much easier to use than any of the plug-ins from the past. The <audio> element supports three audio formats: MP3, WAV, and OGG. Some browsers may not support all file types, just like video, so you may want to provide your sound clips in more than one format. That way the browser can pick the format it can play the best.

The <audio> element works just like a <video> element. Inside the <audio> you place one or more <source> elements listing the filename and type. The web browser will select the audio file type it knows how to play the best. At the bottom you can add a message to show if the web browser does not support the HTML5 <audio> tag.

```
<audio controls>
    <source src="song.ogg" type="audio/ogg">
    <source src="song.mp3" type="audio/mpeg">
    <source src="song.wav" type="audio/wav">
    Your browser does not support the audio tag.
</audio>
```

Inside the <audio> tag you can add several attributes that behave exactly the same as the <video> tag.

<audio> Attribute	Description
autoplay	If present, the audio will start playing as soon as the page loads
controls	If present, the audio frame will include common controls such as play or pause
loop	If present, the audio will play in an endless loop
muted	If present, the audio sound will be turned off
preload	Just like video, audio files can be large, so this option lets you guide how the audio file will be loaded. "*auto*" means load the entire audio right away. "*metadata*" means load only information about the audio, but not the audio itself. "*none*" means don't load anything right away. When the user clicks on the audio to play it, any missing information or files is then loaded.

The most common attribute is **controls**. It displays a control bar for playing, pausing and stopping the playback of the audio file as well as a way to control its volume. Of course there is no image, so all you will see is a track-bar with the play button and other controls. The exact look of the audio element depends on your web browser.

Best Practice

Adding sound or videos to your web site can be a great feature, but keep your reader in mind. It could be a big surprise if your computer suddenly starts making noise when you were quietly browsing, especially if the reader is in a library or other quiet place. It is best practice to set up the audio and video *without* **autoplay**. Instead, let the user click on the play button to hear the audio or play the video clip.

Chapter Review

- Each of the major web browsers has different levels of support for different video formats.

- One easy way to put videos on your web page is to let someone else host them on their computer systems, like YouTube.

- Most browsers used to support the Flash Player plug-in automatically, or you could download the free Flash plug-in from the Adobe website if needed.

- However, the Flash format is (over a long period of time) going to be replaced by newer formats and HTML5.

- To add a Flash movie to a web page, you can use either the <**embed**> element or the <**object**> element anywhere inside the <**body**>.

- All images, videos and sounds you find online are owned by someone, and you need to have permission to use those files.

- If you find a movie online, make sure you carefully read and understand the copyright information before embedding that movie on your own page.

- HTML5 includes a new <**video**> element, which is an easy way to show videos on your web page.

- Inside the <**video**> element you can place one or more <**source**> elements. Each <**source**> represents one video file format.

- The three main video file formats you can use with the <**video**> element are MP4 (type="video/mp4"), OGG (typ="video/ogg"), and WEBM (type="video/webm").

- If a browser can't understand the HTML5 <**video**> tag at all it will show the text underneath the <**source**> elements.

- You can control the way a video will behave inside the browser using several optional attributes.

- You can style the <**video**> element using CSS just like any other HTML element.

- HTML5 includes a new <**audio**> element, which is a great way to play sounds on your page.

- The <**audio**> element works just like a <**video**> element – with multiple possible sources and optional control attributes like "autoplay" and "loop".

- It is best practice to set up the audio and video *without* **autoplay**.

Your Turn Activity: Sound Bites

In this activity you are going to add a several sound clips to your Aquamaniacs web site. You will set up a dedicated "Sound Bites" page where the user can hear recordings of dolphins, penguins, and other creatures.

Your activity requirements and instructions are found in the "Chapter_05_Activity.pdf" document located in your "KidCoder/AdvancedWebDesign/Activity Docs" folder. You can access this document through your Student Menu or by double-clicking on it from Windows Explorer or Mac OS Finder.

Chapter Six: Introducing CSS3

CSS3 is a new version of Cascading Style Sheets that adds many new styling options for your web page. Everything you already know about CSS is still valid, but CSS3 offers more properties and values.

Lesson One: Browser Compatibility

With the development of HTML5 comes a new version of Cascading Style Sheets called "CSS3". You are very comfortable with simple CSS rules by now, so learning CSS3 will be easy! The standard CSS selectors, properties and values are all still included in the new CSS3 standard. The main additions in CSS3 include:

- Special effects like rounded corners, drop shadows, and specialized fonts
- Gradients and multiple background images
- 2D and 3D transformations
- New animation properties
- Styling <**audio**> and <**video**> tags.

Just like HTML5, CSS3 is a developing standard and not all web browsers support all new CSS3 features. But most major browsers will support the most common CSS3 features, and with each release a browser will add in new CSS3 features.

How do you know if your browser works well with CSS3? One easy test can be run at this website:

http://css3test.com/   (Notice there is no "www." on the front)

This website will take a look at your current browser and give you an overall percentage score for the number of CSS3 features that are supported. The 58% score to the right was earned by Mozilla Firefox version 25.0.1.

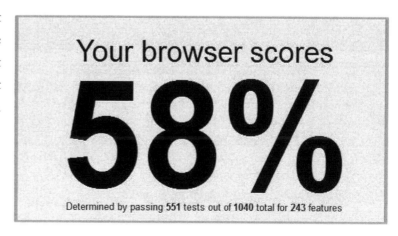

Your browser scores

58%

Determined by passing **551** tests out of **1040** total for **243** features

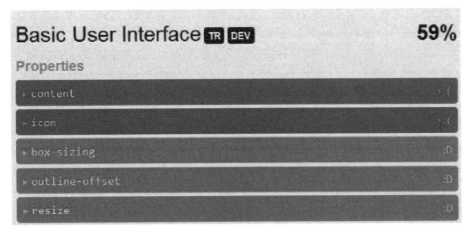

In addition to an overall percentage, the CSS3 test site will give you specific information on each property and value of CSS3 that is or is not supported in your browser.

The web browser you are using should be recent enough to support the HTML5 and CSS3 features we teach in this course. Back in Chapter Two you had a chance to test your browser for HTML5 support, and in a minute you'll get a chance to test CSS3 support as well. If your web browser does not support any of the features we talk about, then it is pretty old and we recommend upgrading as soon as possible.

Cross-Browser Compatibility

Cross-browser compatibility refers to the different ways a web page looks depending on the browser, the version of browser, or the operating system on your computer. These issues affect all web designers, which is why you are encouraged to always check your web site in a variety of browsers. Hopefully HTML5 support will make websites more consistent, but as long as older browsers are around, there is still a chance your web page will look different in different browsers. Consider this page shown in 3 browsers:

Styling is exactly correct	The big "D" letter is dropped down too far.	The big "D" letter is missing a text shadow and is dropped down too far.

You may have to add extra style rules to get the exact behavior you want in most web browsers.

Graceful Degradation and Progressive Enhancement

If you assume that most of your website users are using new browsers that support most HTML5 and CSS3 features, but take a few extra steps to make the site basically functional with older browsers, then you are practicing **graceful degradation**. On the other hand, if you assume that most of your users are using older browsers without HTML5 and CSS3 support, and you add in a few extra nice features that newer browsers can use, then you are using a concept called **progressive enhancement**.

If you think about it, both graceful degradation and progressive enhancement are really the same thing, it's just a matter of your starting assumptions. In both cases you are trying to make your website work very well for the most number of users and still function for the smaller set of users with different browsers. Since some users are just slow to upgrade browsers to the latest versions, you may want to live without some of the newest HTML5 or CSS3 features so your site works well for everyone.

In some cases an older version of a web browser implemented a CSS3 feature very early as an experiment. You can add extra properties for these specific browsers to use their experimental support for CSS3 instead of the standard properties. For example, if you use the "-moz-" prefix on some CSS3 properties, older versions of Mozilla Firefox might support the property with that non-standard name. In the example below we use a standard CSS3 property called **border-radius** (that you'll learn about soon). We also added the "-moz-" version in case an older Firefox browser happens to use our site.

```
border-radius:25px;
-moz-border-radius:25px; /* Old Firefox */
```

Successful support for graceful degradation and progressive enhancement is a fairly large task for public or commercial websites. We'll assume your web browser is new enough to handle the HTML5 and CSS3 features we're learning about in this course, but keep these topics in mind as you continue working with website designs.

Work with Me: Check Your Browser CSS3 Compatibility

Take a minute and check your computer's web browser for CSS3 compatibility.

1. Open the web browser you are using for this course.
2. Enter the address: http://css3test.com.
3. How well does your browser score? Recent versions of most major browsers will probably score over 50%, but you probably won't find any browser with close to 100%.
4. If you have more than one web browser installed on your computer, compare the scores for each.

If your browser scores very poorly or does not support individual CSS3 features you learn about in this course, you may want to update your browser to the latest version or consider installing another browser.

Lesson Two: Colors and Transparency

In this lesson, we will take a look at some of the newer CSS3 properties that are used to handle the colors and transparency on your web page.

The "opacity" Property

"Opacity" is a fancy word describing how much light something will allow to shine through. You can use the CSS3 **opacity** property with values between 0.0 and 1.0 to make an element (and everything inside it) partially transparent. The effect is like sheer curtains that you can see through a little bit to see what is behind them. In this example we have assigned an **opacity** of 1.0 to an element.

```
#MainContent {
    background: url(mouse-running.jpg) left top no-repeat;
    opacity: 1.0;
}
```

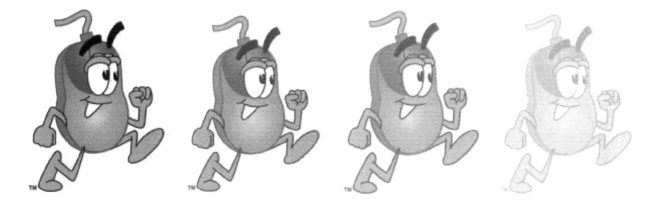

The image on the left is fully visible with an **opacity** of 1.0. But as we reduce the **opacity** down to 0.7, 0.5, and 0.2, the image begins to fade away, showing more and more of whatever happens to be underneath. Opacity sets the transparency value for an element **and all of its children** so anything inside the styled element will also become transparent.

RGBA Colors

You are familiar with setting colors using hexadecimal numbers for the Red, Green, and Blue components.

```
color: #CCCCCC;  /* a light gray color */
```

Each pair of hexadecimal letters represents one color, so in the example above we have Red = #CC, Green = #CC, and Blue = #CC, and the resulting color is a light gray.

You can also set colors using regular decimal numbers 0 – 255 for each component. Instead of a pound sign (#), use the "**rgb()**" syntax instead:

```
color: rgb(204, 204, 204);  /* a light gray color */
       (red) (green) (blue)
```

With CSS3 you can also use RGBA colors, where the "A" stands for the "alpha" channel. The alpha value controls the transparency of the color. The value for alpha ranges from 0.0, which is fully transparent, to 1.0 which is completely solid.

```
color: rgb(0, 0, 0, 0.6);  /* also a light gray color */
       (red) (green) (blue) (alpha)
```

Let's see some examples in action!

```
<p style="color: #CCCCCC;">What color am I?</p>
<p style="color: rgb(204, 204, 204);">What color am I?</p>
<p style="color: rgba(0, 0, 0, 1.0);">What color am I?</p>
<p style="color: rgba(0, 0, 0, 0.6);">What color am I?</p>
```

The top line uses some standard hexadecimal values for light gray. Next we convert those same values into decimal **rgb()**, so the first two lines appear to be exactly the same shade. In the third line we use an all-black selection of **rgba()** with an **alpha** of 1.0, so the black is completely solid. Finally, we use the same **rgba()** black but reduce the **alpha** to 0.6, so the black color appears to fade out.

What color am I?

What color am I?

What color am I?

What color am I?

Unlike the opacity setting, a **rgba()** color property controls the transparency for just that color, so children of the element are not impacted.

Color Shortcuts

Hexadecimal colors contain 3 pairs of 2 numbers for each of the Red, Green, and Blue components like #00FFAA. If within every pair such as #00, #FF, and #AA, the letters or numbers are the same, then you can use a "shortcut" to write the values. The shortcut uses just one letter or number for each pair, so our example could be written as #0FA. Any web browser seeing just 3 digits for a color will automatically expand them by copying each digit twice. So #0FA would expand back to #00FFAA to make the real color. You cannot shorten the notation unless Red, Green and Blue values **all** are made of doubles. For example, #AAABCC cannot be shortened. The most common color shortcuts you will see are for black #000, white #FFF, and gray #CCC.

Work with Me: Transparent Whales

It's time to test out your transparency skills. We are going to add a new page called "Whales.html" to your Aquamaniacs site, and then apply some styles in the "global.css" file.

To begin, copy the "whales.html" file from your "Activity Starters/ Chapter06" directory into your "MyProjects/Aquamaniacs" folder. Then load the "whales.html" file into your web browser to see the initial view as shown to the right.

To start this page just shows a plain list of facts. If you look at the

Killer Whales

live in groups called pods

black body, white lower jaw and belly, and white patch directly behind the eye

are the largest member of the dolphin family

a newborn calf averages 8 ft (2.4 m) in length

are the fastest swimming mammal

communicate with clicks and whistles

eat fish, marine mammals, sea turtles, and birds

are found in all the worlds oceans - hot and cold

are considered to be an endangered species

"whales.html" source code in Komodo Edit, you will find the "MainContent" **<div>** has a headline and an internal "taskbox" **<div>**. Each **<p>** has a "block1" or "block2" class in an alternating pattern.

```
<div id="MainContent">
    <h1>Killer Whales</h1>
    <div id="taskbox">
      <p class="block1">live in groups called pods</p>
      <p class="block2">black body, white lower jaw and belly, and white patch
directly behind the eye</p>
      <p class="block1">are the largest member of the dolphin family</p>
      <p class="block2">a newborn calf averages 8 ft (2.4 m) in length</p>
      <!-- other lines here, but skipped to keep it short -->
    </div>
</div><!-- end of MainContent -->
```

Now, load "global.css" into Komodo Edit and scroll down to the bottom. All of the work you need to do for this "Work with Me" will be in "global.css".

1. At the **bottom** of "global.css", add the following two CSS rules. The first rule will set the overall width of the "taskbox" <**div**> to 600 pixels. The second rule will make each "block1" and "block2" paragraph appear as a 120 x 120 pixel box with a solid border and some text styles. The blocks will float left, so the browser will arrange them as neatly as possible in the available space.

```
#taskbox{
    width: 600px;
}
.block1,.block2{
    width: 120px;
    height:120px;
    margin:10px;
    padding: 5px;
    font-size: 12px;
    font-weight: bold;
    text-align: center;
    line-height: 18px;
    float: left;
    border:2px solid #CCCCCC;
}
```

Killer Whales

live in groups called pods	black body, white lower jaw and belly, and white patch directly behind the eye	are the largest member of the dolphin family
a newborn calf averages 8 ft (2.4 m) in length	are the fastest swimming mammal	communicate with clicks and whistles
eat fish, marine mammals, sea turtles, and birds	are found in all the worlds oceans - hot and cold	are considered to be an endangered species

2. Save your "global.css" changes and reload "whales.html" in your browser to see the new boxes.

3. Next, in "global.css" at the bottom add two new style rules, one for "block1" and one for "block2" paragraphs. We are setting each group of blocks to a different text color and background color. In addition, all "block1" elements will have an **opacity** of 0.4.

```
.block1{
    color: #717B32;
    background-color: rgb(113,123,50);
    opacity:0.4;
}

.block2{
    color: #BBE1C1;
    background-color: rgba(187,225,193,0.4);
}
```

4. Save your changes and reload "whales.html" in your browser again. You should see that the blocks have a pattern of colors, and the text right now is actually hard to read. That's OK because we are going to change the colors when the user hovers a mouse over each box.

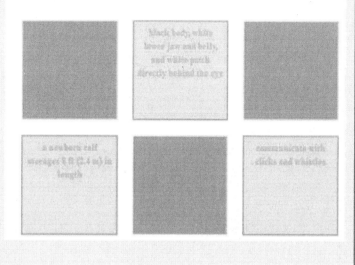

5. As the last step, at the end of "global.css" add two final style rules for "block1" and "block2" that will only take effect when the ":hover" state is enabled.

```
.block1:hover{
    color: black;
    opacity:1.0;
    cursor: default;
}
.block2:hover{
    color: black;
    background-color: rgba(187,225,193,1);
    cursor: default;
}
```

The first rule will change the "block1" text color to black and change the opacity from 0.4 (partially transparent) to 1.0 (solid). The second rule changes the "block2" text color to black and the background to a darker green. In both cases when you over the mouse over a block the text should pop out and be easy to read. We added the **cursor** property to keep the mouse pointer as the *default* while hovering.

Here are examples where the mouse is hovering over "block1" (on the left) and a "block2" (on the right).

Lesson Three: Advanced Borders and Shadows

Border Shorthand Property

You have learned how to control the borders around elements with the **border-style**, **border-width**, and **border-color** properties. Instead of writing those three properties separately, you can combine all of them on the same line as the **border** shorthand property. The **border** will let you set all properties at once for all 4 sides. You can also use this same shorthand pattern with individual border edges such as **border-left** or **border-bottom**.

```
border: 2px solid blue;
border-bottom: thick dotted green;
                (width) (style) (color)
```

The example above will set all 4 **border** sides to a 2 pixel solid blue border. Then the **border-bottom** property will override the values just for the bottom, building a thick dotted green border instead.

The "border-radius" Property (Rounded Corners)

CSS3 offers us an easy way to make fancy, rounded corners on your elements. You can set the **border-radius** property to a value such as 25px or a percentage such as 10%.

```
border: 2px solid blue;
border-radius: 10px;
```

Larger radius pixel values will produce more rounding on the corners. The first example to the right shows a 10px radius. If you use a percentage instead, the entire shape will become more oval-like. The second example shows a radius of 50%.

It's important to understand that the **border-radius** is applied to the entire element, not just a border. You can even set a **border-radius** with no border at all, and the whole element will follow the setting.

```
color: white;
background-color: blue;
border-radius: 25px;
```

In this example we just set a blue background and white text with a **border-radius** of 25px. We will use this property to add some nice effects to our Aquamaniacs website.

The "box-shadow" Property

Another new addition with CSS3 is the **box-shadow** property. This new feature allows you to add shadows to boxes. Basically any element such as a paragraph <p> or <div> that can have a border can also have a box shadow. This property combines several values together.

```
box-shadow: h-shadow v-shadow blur spread color inset;
```

The **h-shadow** and **v-shadow** values are required. These values control how large of a shadow is cast in the horizontal and vertical directions.

```
box-shadow: 5px 10px;
```

In this example we set only a 5px horizontal shadow and a 10px vertical shadow as shown to the right. You can use negative numbers if you want the shadow to go up and the left. The second example uses -5px -10px shadows.

Check out my shadow

Check out my shadow

The optional **blur** value is set in pixels also and will make the edges of the shadow fuzzy instead of crisp.

```
box-shadow: 5px 10px 5px;
```

Check out my shadow

The optional **spread** setting makes the shadow larger than normal.

```
box-shadow: 5px 10px 5px 5px;
```

Check out my shadow

You can change the color of the shadow with the optional **color** value.

```
box-shadow: 5px 10px 5px 5px blue;
```

Check out my shadow

Finally, you can use the optional **inset** value to make the shadow appear reversed inside the element instead of outside.

```
box-shadow: 5px 10px inset;
```

Check out my shadow

Of course, with all shadow effects, you may need to add some internal **padding** to make sure the shadows don't block any content inside.

 **Work with Me: Styling the MainContent <div>**

Each of your Aquamaniacs web pages has a **<div id= "MainContent">** area where the central content is shown. Right now this **<div>** has a plain white background, so let's spice it up with some colors, rounded borders, and a shadow!

1. Run Komodo Edit and open your "global.css" file. Find your existing "#MainContent" rule and get ready to add some more properties. The rule currently contains 3 properties:

```css
#MainContent {
    float: right;
    width: 70%;
    margin-left: 10px;


}
```

2. Remove the existing **margin-left** property and add the following new properties to "#MainContent".

```css
#MainContent {
    float: right;
    width: 70%;
    margin-left: 10px;
    margin: 15px 5px 15px 15px;
    padding: 15px;
    border:2px solid #CCC;
    border-radius:25px;
    box-shadow: 8px 8px 7px rgba(0, 0, 0, 0.6);
    background-color:rgba(198,207,146,0.8);

}
```

3. Save your "global.css" changes and load your main "index.html" file to see the results.

Welcome to Aquamaniacs

Our oceans hold many wild and wonderful sea creatures. Here, you can learn about large animals like whales, dolphins, and sharks. See oddities like the sea urchin, longhorn cowfish, emperor penguin, lobster, lionfish, cuttlefish, and seahorse. Don't forget to visit the octopus and otter!

Follow our navigation links to learn about *"Big Critters"*. Check out the crazy things hidden under the *"Oddballs"* category. Enter our "Multimedia" lab for photos, sounds, and videos. Don't forget to see our *"Animation"* area for some funny effects!

What a difference a few lines of CSS can make! Your main content area on every page should now have a light tan color with rounded borders and a small shadow. Click through the other pages you have created so far such as "Whales", and "Dolphins". Not all of your navigation links work yet, because we haven't created all of the pages. But for those pages we already have, you should see the same nice effects on every page. You are going to use the same 25px **border-radius** later on to round out many of the other square boxes on your website.

If your main content area suddenly appears below the navigation bar, try making your web browser wider. The main content is a bit wider now with the shadows and other effects, so it might not fit to the right side of the navigation bar in a small window. Don't worry about that for now, because we'll eventually move the navigation bar to the top and have plenty of space underneath for the main content.

Lesson Four: Custom Fonts

"Fonts" are collections of letters all written with the same style. You have learned that certain fonts such as "Times New Roman", "Arial", "Courier New", and "Comic Sans MS" are commonly installed on all computers. If you tried to use a fancy font that is not installed on the user's computer, your web page would not look like you wanted. So you were encouraged to use a **font-family** with one or more of these browser-safe fonts so your web page would look the same everywhere. Fortunately, CSS3 has a new way to let you show any font on your web page, even if that font is not already on your user's computer!

Finding Fonts

The Internet contains many places where you can download new fonts. However, some of these places are in the business of **selling** font files and not giving them away. So you need to very carefully read the licensing information about each font before you download and begin using it on your website.

One of the better places to find new fonts is a web site called "Font Squirrel" (http://www.fontsquirrel.com). Font Squirrel finds quality **freeware** fonts that are licensed for commercial work and lists them on their web site. They also have hundreds of prepackaged font kits that contain everything you need to install a font successfully. The new fonts you will add to your Aquamaniacs website are called "Sigmar" and Architects Daughter", and they both come from Font Squirrel.

SIGMAR

Architects Daughter

Licensing

If you are going to use a custom font, make sure its license permits use on a website. If the license agreement isn't clear, it is better to use a different font. Good web sites, like Font Squirrel, will make it easy to find the license. If you want to use the font on your web site, you need to look for statements that clearly state you can use the font on the Internet and you can use it on an unlimited number of computers. The license should contain phrases similar to the examples below.

- "This FONT PACKAGE may be distributed ONLY via the Internet for FREE."
- "You may install and use this FONT PACKAGE on an unlimited amount of machines."

If you want to use the font for print work and other projects, as well as a web site, you need to look for a license that allows use in all areas. Look for phrases that refer to unlimited use and redistribution rights similar to the examples below.

- "The OFL allows the licensed fonts to be used, studied, modified and redistributed freely as long as they are not sold by themselves."
- "This font is freeware, to be downloaded and used by anyone who wants them for free."
- "Creative Commons Attribution Share Alike license… to copy, distribute and transmit the work"

If the license allows you to use a font, it is a nice courtesy to add a comment in your HTML or CSS code that points to the license for the font.

 Some fonts tease you into downloaded the files for free, but the license means you must buy the font to use it on a web site or other project. Remember to check the font license before using it!

Font Files and Browser Support

All newer, major browsers have very good support for custom fonts. Unfortunately, each browser might require a different type of font file format. There are currently four different font formats that must be included in order to target all browsers: TTF, WOFF, EOT and SVG. Often a font will originally be found only in a single format such as TTF. Fortunately, Font Squirrel provides a tool called "Webfont Generator" that will create all four file types from a single source file and also give you the exact CSS needed to create your font in your website. We provide all four file versions for the two fonts we use in Aquamaniacs.

We will keep our fonts in a "Fonts" sub-directory underneath our "Aquamaniacs" folder. So in that directory for a single font such as Sigmar you would find 5 files:

- "SigmarOne-webfont.eot"
- "SigmarOne-webfont.svg"
- "SigmarOne-webfont.ttf"
- "SigmarOne-webfont.woff"
- "Sigmar One SIL OFL Font License.txt"

It's convenient to keep the font license file with the other font files so you always have it handy if asked.

Defining a Custom Font with "@font-face"

Using a custom font on your website is a two-step process. First, in your CSS file, you must define the font by giving it a name and pointing to the files that contain the font information. Once the font is defined, you can then use your new font name in the **font-family** property just like Arial or any other standard font.

To define a font in your CSS, you will create a style rule with **"@font-face"** as the selector. Inside this rule you will add a **font-family** property to define the name, and then one or more **src** properties to connect to each of the font files you have on your system. It's easiest to add this definition at the top of your "global.css" file so the new font name is visible everywhere in your website.

```
@font-face {
    font-family: 'SigmarRegular';
    src: url('../Fonts/SigmarOne-webfont.eot');
    src: url('../Fonts/SigmarOne-webfont.eot?#iefix') format('embedded-
                                                    opentype'),
        url('../Fonts/SigmarOne-webfont.woff') format('woff'),
        url('../Fonts/SigmarOne-webfont.ttf') format('truetype'),
        url('../Fonts/SigmarOne-webfont.svg#SigmarRegular') format('svg');
    font-weight: normal;
    font-style: normal;
}
```

This looks a little complicated, but fortunately all of it is written for you if you use the Font Squirrel Webfont Generator tool. So you'll just have to copy and paste it into your own "global.css".

The **font-family** property within this rule gives your custom font a unique name that you will use throughout your website. In this example, we have created a font named "*SigmarRegular*". Your life will be a lot easier if you do not use any spaces in your **font-family** value.

The **src** attributes point to the location of the font files on your system and describes the file format. You may have to change each of these paths if you are not storing your font files in the same directory as the CSS. Notice above that we have added a relative path "../Fonts/" in front of each URL that will lead up from our "Aquamaniacs/SiteStyle" folder and into the "Aquamaniacs/Fonts" folder.

You can control other parts of the font appearance using properties such as **font-weight** and **font-style** to make a bold or italic font. We have left these values as "*normal*" to get a standard look.

Applying Custom Font Families

Once you have created your new font family name such as "SigmarRegular", you can then use that anywhere else later in your CSS file where you need to set a **font-family**.

You could style the entire body, or just a headline, or a paragraph with individual rules:

```
body {
    font-family: SigmarRegular;
}
h1 {
    font-family: SigmarRegular;
}
p {
    font-family: SigmarRegular;
}
```

You can also use a "group" selector to easily combine rules for different elements like this:

```
h1, h2, h3 {
    font-family: SigmarRegular;
}
```

Just list each element name in the selector separated by a comma. Now all of our <h1>, <h2>, and <h3> elements will use the *SigmarRegular* font. When grouping elements together in a selector, it's best practice to place the group rules higher in your CSS than any other individual rules for one of those elements.

Work with Me: Adding "Sigmar" Font Headlines

We want to add the custom Sigmar font to our Aquamaniacs website exactly as described in the lesson. The Sigmar font will be used for all headlines **<h1>**, **<h2>**, and **<h3>**. We are going to create a new "Sharks" page at the same time to test our fonts.

1. First, copy the "sharks.html" file from your "Activity Starters/Chapter06" directory to your "Aquamaniacs" folder using Windows Explorer or Mac OS Finder.

2. Load the "Aquamaniacs/sharks.html" file into your web browser to see the "before" styling. The page contains three articles, each with an internal headline **<h2>** and a paragraph **<p>**.

We are going to change all of the header elements to use a new font.

Sharks

Nurse Shark

The Nurse shark, one of the more docile members of the shark family, is usually found at the bottom of the ocean, but not too deep. It prefers shallower water around 1 meter deep but will go down as far as 12 meters. This nocturnal creature is usually inactive during the day, often sleeping piled one on top of each other on the sea floor. At night, it hunts by itself for fish, shrimp, sea urchins, the occasional octopus and stingrays. Its fast reactions and stealthy approach make hunting look easy.

Zebra Shark

3. Use Windows Explorer, Mac OS Finder, or Komodo Edit to create a new folder called "Fonts" underneath your "Aquamaniacs" directory.

4. Using Windows Explorer or Mac OS Finder, copy all of the font files you find in your "Activity starters/Chapter06/Fonts" directory into your new "Aquamaniacs/Fonts" directory. Go ahead and copy both the "Sigmar" files and the "ArchitectsDaughter" files, even though we're just using Sigmar to start. When you are done you should see 10 files in your new "Fonts" directory, including 2 license text files.

Now, run Komodo Edit and open your "global.css" File. At the very top we want to add a **@font-face** definition for the Sigmar font. Because the properties are long, you can cut-and-paste them instead!

5. Open the "Activity Starters/Chapter06/font-face.txt" file in your favorite text editor.

6. Select all of the first **@font-face** definition as shown below and paste it into the top of your "global.css" file.

```css
/* Generated by Font Squirrel (http://www.fontsquirrel.com) */
@font-face {
    font-family: 'SigmarRegular';
    src: url('../Fonts/SigmarOne-webfont.eot');
    src: url('../Fonts/SigmarOne-webfont.eot?#iefix') format('embedded-
opentype'),
        url('../Fonts/SigmarOne-webfont.woff') format('woff'),
        url('../Fonts/SigmarOne-webfont.ttf') format('truetype'),
        url('../Fonts/SigmarOne-webfont.svg#SigmarRegular') format('svg');
    font-weight: normal;
    font-style: normal;
}
/* license agreement at http://www.fontsquirrel.com/license/sigmar */
```

7. Directly below the newly entered **@font-face** rule, add a new rule to style all three headlines **<h1>**, **<h2>**, and **<h3>** as a group. We want to set the **font-family** to "SigmarRegular" to match the name we used inside **@font-face**.

```css
h1, h2, h3 {
    font-family: SigmarRegular;
    font-weight: normal;
}
```

Now when you save your changes and reload "sharks.html" in your web browser, you should see that your **<h1>** and **<h2>** elements have the new Sigmar font. All other text should be unchanged.

While we're working on headline styles, let's add some extra rules for individual <h1>, <h2>, and <h3> elements to give each of them a unique color and size.

8. Add the following three style rules directly below the group rule you just added.

```css
h1, h2, h3 {
    font-family: SigmarRegular;
    font-weight: normal;
}

h1 {
    color: #000000;
    font-size: 1.7em;
}
h2 {
    color: #717B32;
    font-size: 1.2em;
}
h3 {
    color: #000000;
    font-size: 1em;
}
```

When finished, save your changes and reload "sharks.html" in your web browser again. You should see the <h2> element get a bit smaller and use a green color that matches our overall color scheme. The <h1> element won't have much visible difference, and we don't have any <h3> elements to look at right now.

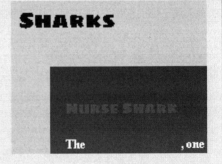

Chapter Review

- CSS3 adds support for special effects like rounded corners, gradients and multiple background images, 2D and 3D transformations, new animation properties and ways to style the new <**audio**> and <**video**> elements.

- You can test your browser's CSS3 compatibility by going to the website at http://css3test.com.

- **Cross-browser compatibility** refers to the different ways a web page looks depending on the browser, the version of browser, or the operating system on your computer.

- Creating a web site that uses the latest HTML and takes a few extra steps to make your site basically functional with older browsers shows you are using *graceful degradation*.

- Creating a web site that uses older HTML, but adds in some newer features for newer browsers is a concept called *progressive enhancement.*

- You can use the CSS3 **opacity** property with values between 0.0 and 1.0 to make an element (and everything inside it) partially transparent.

- In CSS3, you can use the **rgba**() syntax to set red, green, blue and alpha values for a specific color. The alpha value specifies the transparency of the color.

- Instead of writing the **border-style**, **border-width** and **border-color** properties separately, you can combine all of them on the same line as the **border** shorthand property – which will allow you to set all properties at the same time.

- The **border-radius** property allows you to make fancy, rounded corners on your elements.

- The **box-shadow** property allows you to add shadows to boxes.

- "Fonts" are collections of letters all written with the same style.

- The Font Squirrel web site finds quality **freeware** fonts that are licensed for commercial work and lists them on their web site.

- If you are going to use a custom font, make sure its license permits use on a website.

- There are currently four different font formats that must be included in order to target all browsers: TTF, WOFF, EOT and SVG.

- To define a font in your CSS, you will create a style rule with "**@font-face**" as the selector.

- The **font-family** property within this rule gives your custom font a unique name that you will use throughout your website.

Your Turn Activity: Branding Aquamaniacs

In this activity you are going to use a combination of custom fonts and advanced borders to improve your Aquamaniacs website brand.

Your activity requirements and instructions are found in the "Chapter_06_Activity.pdf" document located in your "KidCoder/AdvancedWebDesign/Activity Docs" folder. You can access this document through your Student Menu or by double-clicking on it from Windows Explorer or Mac OS Finder.

Complete this activity now and ensure you understand the material before continuing!

Chapter Seven: Cool CSS3 Features

CSS3 offers many new cool ways to control your images and colors. In this chapter you'll learn about some advanced backgrounds, color gradients, and image transformations.

Lesson One: Advanced Backgrounds

CSS3 gives you several new properties to help control the appearance of images in your background. We will focus on the most useful of these, the **background-size** property.

The "background-size" Property

In earlier versions of CSS, your background images would appear on your page at the natural size of the original image. If your image was 100 pixels wide and 200 pixels tall, it would appear at that size on the page. If you wanted to cover the entire page, you would need a large image that could have a big file size.

Let's consider a page that is 500 pixels high. We'll add a background image to the <**body**> element with a simple rule that specifies no repeating and centering at the bottom edge of the page. Our "mouse-peeking.jpg" image is 300px wide and 253px high, so without any other styles it will appear as shown below.

```
body {
    background: #FFFFFF url(mouse-peeking.png) no-repeat bottom;
}
```

CSS3 introduces the **background-size** property to control the size of the background image using pixels, percentages or some special keywords. You can use this property to stretch or shrink an image to fit exactly into your element.

The **background-size** property can take four different types of values as shown below: *Length*, or *percentage*, "*cover*", or "*contain*".

```
background-size: length|percentage|cover|contain;
```

If you want to use a certain length, you can set the value in pixels. The first number is the width and the second is the height. You can also use the keyword *"auto"* to make the browser figure out one size based on the other. It's easy to distort (stretch or squish) an image if you aren't careful!

```
body {
    background: #FFFFFF url(mouse-peeking.png) no-repeat bottom;
    background-size: auto 350px;
}
```

Here we have set the **background-size** to use a *350px* height and automatically calculate the width. You can see the resulting image is larger even though we didn't change the original file size.

Instead of a pixel value you could use a percentage instead. A value of **100%** will stretch to entirely cover the element you are styling, as shown to the right.

```
background-size: auto 100%;
```

Finally, there are a couple of keywords you can use instead of a pixel or percentage value. The *"contains"* value will scale up the image as large as possible without cutting off any part of the image. Let's switch to a long, wide image to see how this works.

```
body {
    background: #FFFFFF url(mouse-lying.png) no-repeat bottom;
    background-size: contains;
}
```

Because this image was wider than it was high, it was scaled up until the width matches the element width. That leaves some empty space at the top, but you can see the whole image.

The *"cover"* value, instead, will scale up the image using the smaller of the width or height until it covers the entire element. That means some part of your image will probably be cut off.

Multiple Backgrounds

CSS3 allows you to use more than one background image at the same time. You simply add more than one "url" value on the **background-image** property separated by commas as shown below.

```
body {
    background-image:url(mouse-lying.png),url(mouse-peeking.png);
    background-repeat: no-repeat;
    background-position: bottom;
}
```

The resulting images are layered on top of each other, with the first declaration on top, the second below it, the third below that one, and so on. You can see to the right that our "lying" mouse is on top of the "peeking" mouse image because it was listed first. Now, it doesn't make much sense to layer these two images on top of each other because it just makes a mess. But you might find other images that work well together when layered into the same background.

Work with Me: Adding the Octopus Background

As part of our overall style, we want a neat image of an octopus to appear in the background of the main <**body**> area. Follow these steps put this image in the bottom right corner:

1. Using Windows Explorer or Mac OS Finder, copy the "octopus.png" file from "Activity Starters/Chapter07/SiteStyle" directory to your "Aquamaniacs/SiteStyle" folder.

2. Open "global.css" in Komodo Edit and add a new rule for the <**body**> near the top. Place this rule above all other style rules, but below the two **@font-face** declarations.

```
/* license agreement at http://www.fontsquirrel.com/license/architects-
daughter */


body {
    font-family: Verdana, Helvetica, Arial, sans-serif;
    color: #000000;
    font-size: 0.9em;
    font-weight: normal;
    padding: 0;
    margin: 0;
    background: #FFFFFF url(octopus.png) no-repeat right bottom;
    background-size: contain;
}

p {
```

This rule is setting the defaults for all elements in the body! In cases where you have rules for more specific elements like <**p**>, <**h1**>, or <**article**>, those more specific rules will take effect. But anywhere not already covered by a rule will follow the main <**body**> styles.

The <**body**> rule is setting the default font family, color, size, and weight. It removes all padding and margins. The biggest change is the addition of a white background with an "octopus.png" image that will float to the bottom-right corner without repeating. By setting the **background-size** property to "**contain**", we also tell the browser to automatically scale the image up as large as possible to fill the body without cutting off any part of the image.

When you are finished, save your "global.css" and load up several of your website pages in the web browser. You should see a cool octopus lurking in the bottom right corner of every web page! You can see an example on the next page.

This image shows the main body area of the "index.html" home page.

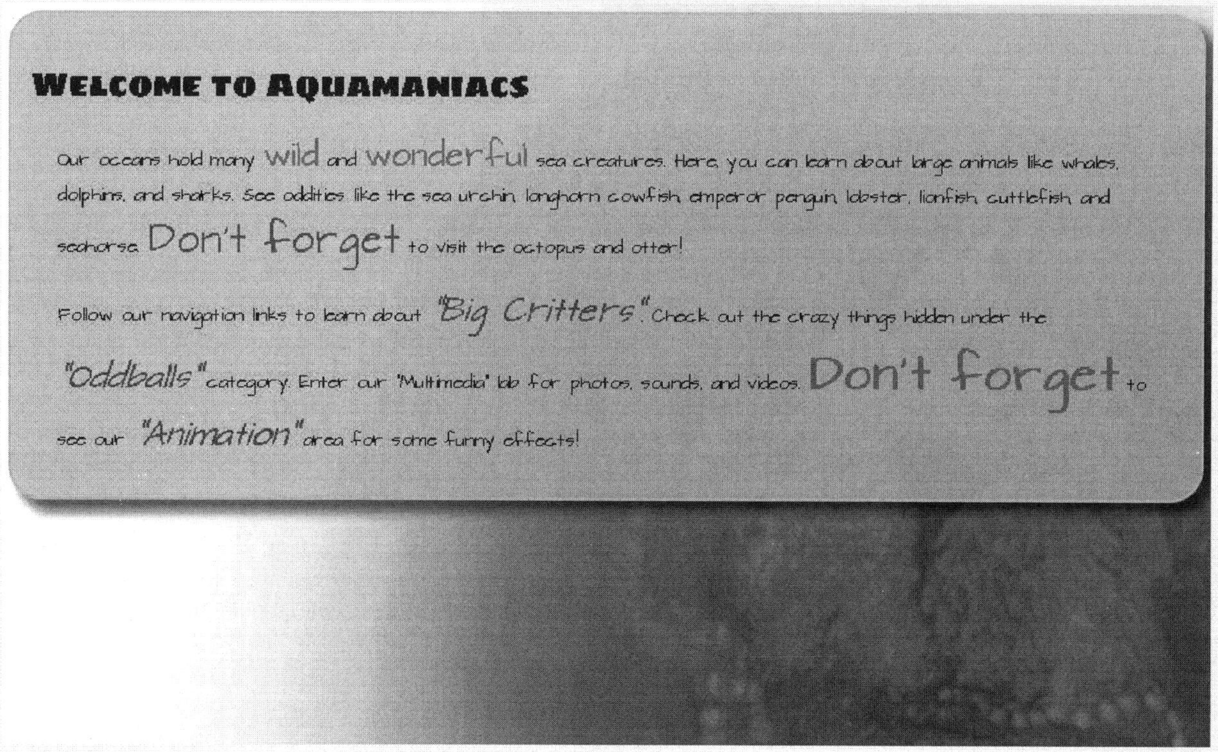
WELCOME TO AQUAMANIACS
Our oceans hold many wild and wonderful sea creatures. Here, you can learn about large animals like whales, dolphins, and sharks. See oddities like the sea urchin, longhorn cowfish, emperor penguin, lobster, lionfish, cuttlefish and seahorse. Don't forget to visit the octopus and otter!
Follow our navigation links to learn about "Big Critters". Check out the crazy things hidden under the "Oddballs" category. Enter our "Multimedia" lab for photos, sounds, and videos. Don't forget to see our "Animation" area for some funny effects!

Lesson Two: Gradients

Gradients are smooth transitions between two or more colors. This blending of colors is a great way to add a special look to your web page without having to load large graphic files. CSS3 has built-in support for different types of gradients. Wherever you would normally use a "url(image name)" in a **background-image** or **background** shortcut property, you can place a gradient instead.

Simple Linear and Radial Gradients

The two main types of gradients are "**linear**" and "**radial**". Linear gradients change colors in a straight line from top to bottom, left to right, or other line at any angle. Radial gradients on the other hand start with one color in the middle and expand outwards, changing colors in a circle or ellipse pattern.

To create a gradient, the value for the **background-image** property begins with either **linear-gradient** or **radial-gradient**, followed by starting and ending colors separated by commas inside parentheses.

```
background: linear-gradient(starting color, ending color)
background: radial-gradient(starting color, ending color)
```

Keep in mind you can apply the **background-image** or **background** properties to most elements, and the resulting image or gradient pattern will appear in the background behind any content for that element. Let's use a CSS3 rule for a **<div>** element to show a simple example of a linear and radial gradient.

```
div {
    background: linear-gradient(yellow,blue);
}
```

```
div {
    background: radial-gradient(yellow,blue);
}
```

In the top linear example we have selected yellow and blue, so the linear gradient starts at the top with the first color (yellow) and blends into the second color (blue). The bottom radial example shows how the first color starts in the middle and then blends outward in a circle towards the second color.

Gradients are a very new CSS3 property and may look somewhat different on each type of browser. Internet Explorer does not support gradients at all until version 10, so if you are using IE 9 or earlier you will need to upgrade your browser in order to see these effects on your computer. Older browsers of all types may not show gradients at all.

Gradients with More than Two Colors

Simple gradients with two colors are neat, but why not try for three or more? You can list as many colors as you want, just separate the colors by a comma, like this:

```
div {
    background: linear-gradient(yellow,orange,green,blue,pink,purple);
}
```

You can do the same thing with radial gradients.

```
div {
    background: radial-gradient(yellow,orange,green,blue,pink,purple);
}
```

If you are reading a black and white textbook, it's hard to see what's going on with the different colors. Don't worry; you'll get a chance to see the real thing on your computer!

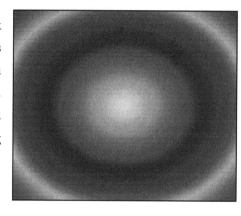

Color Stop Positions

You can control how much each color spreads across the screen before it is fully blended into another color. These settings are called "**color stop positions**". You can set a different stop position for each color.

A color stop position is stated as a percentage of the total gradient. The start of the gradient is located at 0%, the middle of the gradient is located at 50% and the end is located at 100%. This means that a color stop position of 20% would be near the start and a value of 80% would be near the end of the gradient.

Let's experiment with a 70% color stop set on our first color. That means the first color will cover about 70% (or more than half) of the screen before the second color starts kicking in.

```
div {
    background: linear-gradient(yellow 70%, blue);
}
```

```
div {
    background: radial-gradient(yellow 70%, blue);
}
```

If you wanted the second color to take up most of the screen, you could set a small color stop (say 20% or 30%) on that second color. That would cause the second color to start at that earlier location. You can assign a different stop position to each color, even if you are using more than 2 colors. Just make sure that each percentage value as you move down your list is **greater than or equal to** the one before, because each color must start at a location **after** the one before it.

```
div {
    background: radial-gradient(yellow 50%, blue 50%, white 80%, green 80%);
}
```

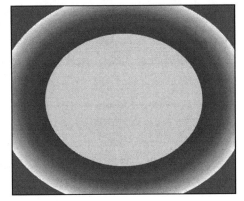

Two side-by-side colors can have the same percentage, which makes a sharp, clean line between the colors instead of a gradient. You can see two such lines in the example to the left.

Of course you don't need to set any color stop positions at all. By default the web browser will spread each color evenly across the screen.

Linear Gradient Direction

By default, the direction of a linear gradient is top to bottom on the screen. However, you can change this with a direction value. The direction value can be either **an angle** which the gradient should follow or the **side or corner** where the gradient should go.

The direction keywords are "**to top**", "**to bottom**", "**to left**" and "**to right**". You can also choose a corner with a combination such as "**to bottom right**". Just place these keywords at the beginning of your color list, separated by a comma.

```
div {
    background: linear-gradient(to right,
                               yellow, blue);
}
```

```
div {
    background: linear-gradient(to bottom right,
                               yellow, blue);
}
```

If you use an angle value instead, the angle would be a number between 0 and 360 written with "deg" at the end such as "0deg" or "45deg". You can use negative numbers as well like "-30deg". The angle controls the difference between a horizontal (straight across) line and the line of the gradient. It's easiest to experiment on your own to see how different angle values control the direction of the gradient.

Radial Center Position

Normally a radial gradient will start in the center and spread out evenly towards the edges. But you can set the starting position of the center of the gradient using keywords like "**at left**", "**at top**", "**at right**" and "**at bottom**". You can set a corner with a combination of keywords such as "**at top right**" or "**at bottom left**".

In this example we set the **top left** corner as the starting point for our radial gradient. We also added some color stops that are not too far apart so the line between colors is easier to see.

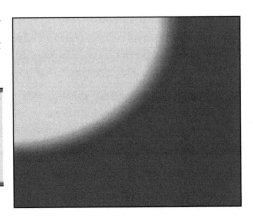

```
div {
    background: radial-gradient(at top left,
                yellow 45%, blue 55%);
}
```

Work with Me: Groovy Fish Gradients

Let's work with some gradients on a new Aquamaniacs page called "Groovy Fish". The HTML page has been created for you in the Activity Starters folder, so you just need to copy it into your Aquamaniacs directory and then apply some CSS styles.

1. Using Windows Explorer or Mac OS Finder, copy the "groovyfish.html" file from your "Activity Starters/Chapter07" directory to your "MyProjects/Aquamaniacs" folder.

2. Load the "groovyfish.html" file in your web browser to see the default content. To start, the page will just show some lines of text underneath the headlines.

CRAZY ENVIRONMENTS

SWIMMING WITH COLORS

Default linear 2 colors
Top Left linear with 4 colors
Positioned linear with overlapping color stops
Default radial with 2 colors
Bottom radial with 3 colors
Positioned radial with 5 color stops

3. Now load the "groovyfish.html" file into Komodo Edit and find the "#MainContent" area. You can see that each line of text is in a **<div>** with a unique ID. You will not have to make any changes to this file; instead we will apply CSS rules against these unique IDs.

```html
<div id="MainContent">
    <h1>Crazy Environments</h1>
    <h2>Swimming with Colors</h2>

    <div id="gradient1">Default linear 2 colors</div>
    <div id="gradient2">Top Left linear with 4 colors</div>
    <div id="gradient3">Positioned linear with overlapping color stops</div>
    <div id="gradient4">Default radial with 2 colors</div>
    <div id="gradient5">Bottom radial with 3 colors</div>
    <div id="gradient6">Positioned radial with 5 color stops</div>
</div><!-- end of MainContent -->
```

4. Now, load the "global.css" file in Komodo Edit and go down to the bottom. Add the following new rule to style all of the "gradient1" through "gradient6" elements. If you don't want to type it all out by hand, you can cut-and-paste from the "Activity Starters/Chapter07/common-gradients.txt" file.

```css
#gradient1,#gradient2,#gradient3,#gradient4,#gradient5,#gradient6{
    width: 150px;
    height: 150px;
    float: left;
    margin: 5px;
    padding: 5px;
    border:2px solid #CCCCCC;
    border-radius:25px;
    box-shadow: 8px 8px 7px
                rgba(0,0,0,0.6);
    font-weight: bold;
    text-align: center;
    font-size: large;
}
```

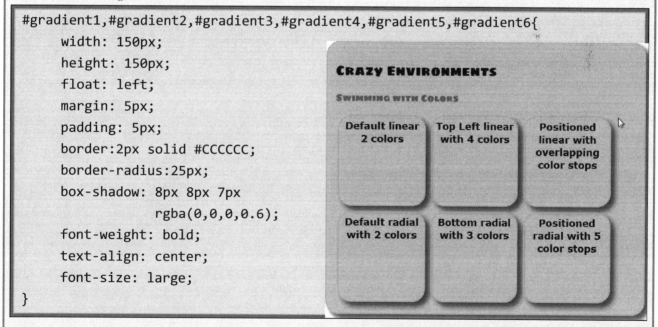

When you save your "global.css" changes and reload "groovyfish.html", you should see each **<div>** is now a nicely rounded and positioned box with bold, centered text.

Each box is going to contain background with a fish image and a gradient. Remember, you can layer backgrounds just by listing them in order, separated by commas. So we will list the image first to put it on top, and the gradient second to put it under the image.

5. Using Windows Explorer or Mac OS Finder, copy the "fish.png" file from "Activity Starters/Chapter07/SiteStyle" to your "Aquamaniacs/SiteStyle" folder.

6. Now, add the following individual style rules for "#gradient1" and "#gradient4" at the bottom of "global.css".

```
#gradient1{
    background-image:url("fish.png"),linear-gradient(red, yellow);
    background-repeat: no-repeat;
    background-position: right bottom;
}


#gradient4{
    background-image:url("fish.png"),radial-gradient(pink,blue);
    background-repeat: no-repeat;
    background-position: right bottom;
}
```

7. When finished. Save your "global.css" and reload "groovyfish.htm;" in your web browser. You should see the two left-hand boxes now contain fish images and a groovy linear or radial gradient!

8. You can experiment with different gradient colors to see what cool effects you can make on your own.

You will complete the remaining 4 gradients as part of the activity at the end of this chapter.

Lesson Three: Image Transformations

CSS3 allows you to transform an element by moving, stretching, skewing, or rotating it in some creative ways. This type of simple animation can help add some interest to your pages and attract readers. We will demonstrate many transformations on a single page. But you will need to use some common sense when thinking about transformations for a public website. Your transformations should be useful and avoid distracting the reader from the main purpose of the page.

Some of these new CSS3 properties are still considered "experimental" and may not be available on all browsers. If you are using an older browser you may need to upgrade in order to see all of the effects. Internet Explorer users must be at version 10 or higher.

Work with Me: Preparing to Transform Funny Fish 1

We are going to set up a new page called "Funny Fish 1" to show image transformations. Follow the steps below to get ready for transforms!

1. Using Windows Explorer or Mac OS Finder, copy the "Activity Starters/Chapter07/funnyfish1.html" file to your "MyProjects/Aquamaniacs" folder.
2. Also copy the four "fish1.jpg" to "fish4.jpg" files from the "Activity Starters/Chapter07/SiteStyle/" to "MyProjects/Aquamaniacs/SiteStyle" folder.
3. Load the "Aquamaniacs/funnyfish1.html" file into your web browser to see the default page.

FUNNY FISH

Translate
Rotate
Scale
Skew

4. Just like our Groovy Fish gradients page, this page contains individual **<div>** elements with unique IDs "fish1" through "fish4". We want to add some style rules to "global.css" to arrange these **<div>** elements into rounded boxes with unique fish images. Because this involves a bunch of typing, it's easier to copy and paste all of the rules from a text file.

    Load the "Activity Starters/Chapter07/common-funnyfish1.txt" file into your favorite text editor. You can see the file contains five rules starting with a group rule and ending with "fish1" through "fish4" rules.

```
#fish1,#fish2,#fish3,#fish4 {

/* all the way through the end of ... */

#fish4 {
```

    Copy the entire set of rules from this text file into the bottom of your "global.css" page.

5. Save your "global.css" changes and load "funnyfish1.html" into your web browser.

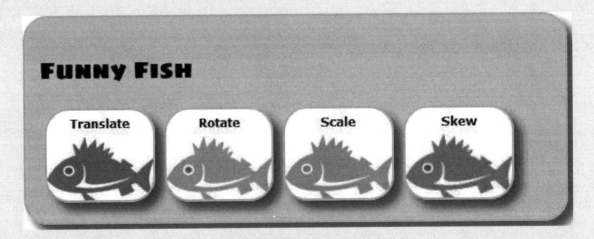

Now each **<div>** should appear as a rounded box with bold, centered text and a different color fish image in each box. In the next section you will start adding transformations to each box using new CSS3 style rules.

The "transform" Property

To apply new CSS3 transformations to an element, you will use the **transform** property. Let's start with a simple <**div**> that contains a background image.

```
div {
    background:url("mouse-peeking.png") bottom no-repeat;
}
```

Now, we can add a transform property to the style rule.

```
div {
    background:url("mouse-peeking.png") bottom no-repeat;
    transform: value
}
```

The type of transformation you get is controlled by the **value** of the **transform** property.

Transform "translate()" Value

You can use the "**translate(X,Y)**" value to move an element from its normal position. The X and Y parameters are the number of pixels to move across from the left and down from the top. For example:

```
div {
    background:url("mouse-peeking.png") bottom no-repeat;
    transform: translate(150px,50px);
}
```

The <**div**> element has moved 150px from the left and 50px from the top.

Transform "rotate()" Value

The transform "**rotate(deg)**" value will spin an element in a clockwise or counterclockwise direction according to the angle given in degrees. Positive values will spin the element in the clockwise direction, while negative values will spin in the counter-clockwise direction. In this example, we have rotated the element 30 degrees clockwise.

```
div {
    background:url("mouse-peeking.png") bottom no-repeat;
    transform: rotate(30deg);
}
```

Transform "scale()" Value

If you want to stretch or shrink an element, you can do this easily with the transform "**scale(X,Y)**" value. The X value will be used to multiply the original width and the Y value will multiply the original height. You can use values less than 1.0 to shrink the image and greater than 1.0 to stretch in a direction.

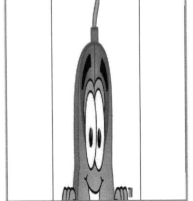

```
div {
    background:url("mouse-peeking.png")
                bottom no-repeat;
    transform: scale(0.5,2.0);
}
```

In this example we used 0.5 for the X scale, so the image is shrunk in the horizontal direction. A 2.0 value for the Y scale means the image is stretched top to bottom.

Transform "skew()" Value

You can "skew" or stretch and tilt an element in a horizontal or vertical direction with the "**skew(X,Y)**" value. Each X and Y component is a positive or negative number given in degrees such as "20deg" or "-40deg". Skewing along the X direction will stretch and tilt the top of the image left or right in relation to the bottom. Skewing in the Y direction will move the right side of the image up or down in relation to the left side. The exact effects are a bit hard to explain in words, so let's see several examples!

```
div {
    background:url("mouse-peeking.png") bottom no-repeat;
    transform: skew(20deg,0deg);
}
```

The image to the right shows a "20deg" skew in the X direction.

We can change to a "20deg" skew in the Y direction to get the image shown to the left.

```
div {
    background:url("mouse-peeking.png") bottom no-repeat;
    transform: skew(0deg,20deg);
}
```

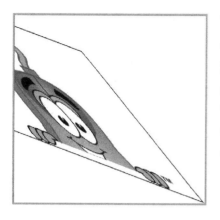

When you combine both an X and Y direction skew the results can be a bit hard to predict. So just try a few different values to see what you get. These two images show a "*skew(40deg,20deg)*" (left) and "*skew(200deg,300deg)*" (right).

Other Great Transforms

We won't have time to cover all of the possible CSS3 transformations. You can rotate an element in 3 dimensions using the "*rotateX()*" and "*rotateY()*" values. You can also make an element grow with a "*transition()*" value. If you are curious about these special effects, you can play with them on your own.

Compatibility with Chrome and Safari

The **transform** property is very new, and not all browsers support this CSS3 property yet. At the moment, Google Chrome and Apple Safari will not recognize the **transform** property, though they may fix this in newer releases of the browsers. Fortunately, these browsers support an experimental version of the property that works the same way.

To make Chrome and Safari work, you need to make a copy of the "transform" line in your CSS file and add the **"-webkit-"** prefix at the beginning.

```
div {
    background:url("mouse-peeking.png") bottom no-repeat;
    transform: skew(0deg,20deg);
    -webkit-transform: skew(0deg,20deg);
}
```

Whenever you use any type of transform (**translate, rotate, scale, skew**), make a copy of that CSS property within your rule and add "**-webkit-**" in the front. Your Google Chrome and Apple Safari users will thank you! If you are using a Chrome or Safari browser for your course work, you must add this prefix to see good results yourself.

Work with Me: Funny Fish 1 Transforms

We want each of the fish on our "Funny Fish 1" page to transform when the user hovers a mouse over the elements. Let's add some rules to our CSS page to make this happen!

1. Open your "global.css" in Komodo Edit

2. Add the following two style rules at the very bottom:

```
#fish1:hover
{
    transform: translate(80px,50px);
    -webkit-transform: translate(80px,50px);
}
#fish2:hover
{
    transform: rotate(40deg);
    -webkit-transform: transform: rotate(40deg);
}
```

3. Save your "global.css" changes and load "funnyfish1.html" in your web browser. The first two fish elements should now move and rotate when you hover the mouse over each element.

4. Experiment with different values for the **translate**() and **rotate**() styles. See how you can move and rotate the elements using different numbers.

Chapter Review

- CSS3 introduces the **background-size** property to control the size of the background image using pixels, percentages or some special keywords.

- CSS3 allows you to use more than one background image at the same time.

- **Gradients** are smooth transitions between two or more colors.

- **Linear** gradients change colors in a straight line from top to bottom, left to right, or other angle.

- **Radial** gradients start with one color in the middle and expand outwards, changing colors in a circle or ellipse pattern.

- You can choose two or more colors to blend into a linear or radial gradient effect.

- You can control how much each color spreads across the screen before it is fully blended into another color with a setting called "**color stop positions**".

- A color stop position is stated as a percentage of the total gradient. The start of the gradient is located at 0%, the middle of the gradient is located at 50% and the end is located at 100%.

- The direction value of a linear gradient can be either **an angle** which the gradient should follow or the **side or corner** where the gradient should travel.

- You can set the starting position of the center of the gradient using keywords like "**at left**", "**at top**", "**at right**" and "**at bottom**".

- CSS3 allows you to transform an element by moving, stretching, skewing, or rotating it in some creative ways.

- To apply new CSS3 transformations to an element, you will use the **transform** property.

- You can use the "**translate(X,Y)**" value to move an element from its normal position.

- The transform "**rotate(deg)**" value will spin an element in a clockwise or counterclockwise direction according to the angle given in degrees.

- The transform "**scale(X,Y)**" value will allow you to stretch or shrink an element.

- The transform "**skew(X,Y)**" value will allow you to "skew" or stretch and tilt an element in a horizontal or vertical direction.

- Google Chrome and Apple Safari do not currently recognize the **transform** property, but support an experimental version of the property by adding "-webkit-" in front of the property name.

Your Turn Activity: Grooving and Shaking

In this activity you are going to finish your new "Groovy Fish" and "Funny Fish 1" pages by adding some gradients and transformations on your own.

Your activity requirements and instructions are found in the "Chapter_07_Activity.pdf" document located in your "KidCoder/AdvancedWebDesign/Activity Docs" folder. You can access this document through your Student Menu or by double-clicking on it from Windows Explorer or Mac OS Finder.

Complete this activity now and ensure you understand the material before continuing!

Chapter Eight: Relationship Selectors

Your CSS style rules are applied to elements on your page identified by the rule's selector. You already know how to use the element name, id, and class to select certain elements on the page. In this chapter you are going to learn some additional ways to select elements based on their relationship or position relative to other elements.

Lesson One: Parent-Child Relationships

Have you heard of "**genealogy**"? This is the study of people and their relatives such as parents, grandparents, brothers, sisters, and children. Often the relationships are drawn in a "**family tree**". One person is placed at the top or bottom of a page. Then, lines are drawn from that person to each parent, and lines from each parent to every grandparent, and so on.

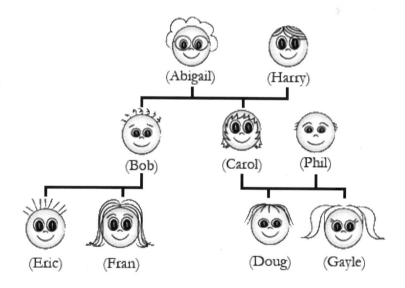

The example to the right shows "Abigail" at the top. Abigail's parents are "Bob" and "Carol", with grandparents "Eric" and "Fran" and "Doug" and "Gayle". Abigail also has a brother "Harry" and an uncle "Phil".

Node Trees

Web pages are very similar to family trees. We can build a "**node tree**" showing the relationships between elements. The outermost <**body**> element is the original parent. Within the <**body**> you will find child elements, grandchildren, great-grandchildren, and so on. The thinking is reversed from a normal family tree where a child is "built" from a combination of parents and other ancestors. On a web page a parent element is "built" from a combination of child elements.

Let's examine a section of our "index.html" page. We are going to focus just on the "MainContent" **<div>** because the overall **<body>** contains a complicated **<nav>** element plus a **<footer>**. When studying element relationships, you can ignore the content (text) inside each element, and just read the HTML tags.

```
<div id="MainContent">
    <h1>Welcome to Aquamaniacs</h1>
    <p>Our oceans hold many <em>wild</em> and <em>wonderful</em> sea creatures.
        Here, you can learn about large animals like whales, dolphins, and
        sharks.  See oddities like the sea urchin, longhorn cowfish, emperor
        penguin, lobster, lionfish, cuttlefish, and seahorse.  <strong>Don't
        forget</strong> to visit the octopus and otter!</p>
    <p>Follow our navigation links to learn about <i>"Big Critters"</i>.  Check
        out the crazy things hidden under the <i>"Oddballs"</i> category.  Enter
        our "Multimedia" lab for photos, sounds, and videos.  <b>Don't forget</b>
        to see our <i>"Animation"</i> area for some funny effects!
    </p>
</div> <!-- end of MainContent -->
```

How would we build a node tree from this HTML, starting with the "MainContent" **<div>** as the root of the tree? We'll place that **<div>** at the top, and then list each child element **<h1>**, **<p>**, and **<p>** underneath. We then look at each child in turn to see if it has any other elements inside. The first paragraph has two **<em>** and one **<strong>** elements, so we list those as children. The second paragraph has two **<i>**, one **<b>**, and another **<i>** so we list those as well at the same level.

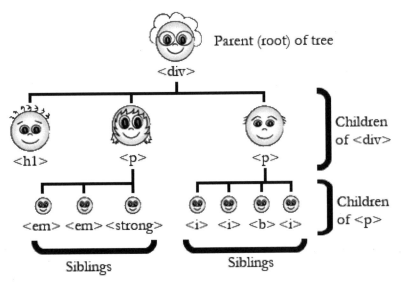

You can see that each element may itself have children, and those children may have other children, and so on. All children that have the same parent are called "**siblings**".

Understanding the relationships between elements on a web page opens up a new level of web design! You can apply CSS rules or run JavaScript commands against specific elements based on their relationships in the overall page.

Notice how you can use careful indentation (spacing) to make child elements appear to the right of parent elements in HTML code? This child <**figure**> tag, for example, is indented inside the parent <**div**> tag.

```
<div>
    <figure></figure>
</div>
```

Indentation and spacing does not actually mean anything to the node tree or DOM though! It's for human readability only, and spacing can be misleading. For example, the following two elements are actually siblings and not in a parent-child relationship – the <**div**> does not contain the <**figure**>.

```
<div></div>
    <figure></figure>
```

Rely only on the opening and closing HTML tags to figure out what elements as parents contain other child elements. A parent element does not contain any children unless those child elements are entirely **in between** the opening and closing parent element tags.

Full Page Example

Let's review another example. The node tree below is based on the full HTML page drawn to the right. The <**html**> node is the top parent and is the largest container on the page. The <**head**> and <**body**> nodes are direct children of <**html**>. Within the <**head**> we have a child <**title**>, and within the body we find a headline <**h1**> and paragraph <**p**>. The paragraph contains three anchor <**a**> links.

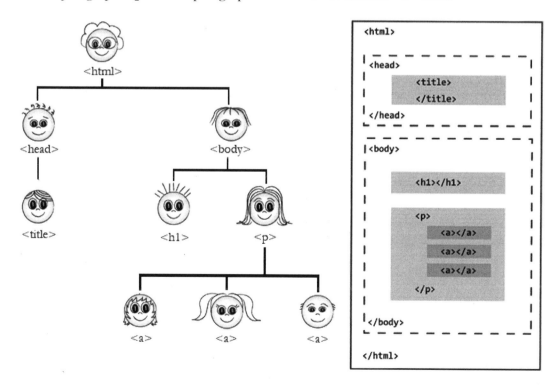

Node Trees and the Document Object Model (DOM)

If you read about web design online, you will likely come across the term "**Document Object Model**" or **DOM**. The DOM is a common way that web browsers will make the contents of a web page available to programming languages like JavaScript. Web designers like to manage the behavior of specific elements on a web page, and the DOM gives a common way across all web browsers to access individual elements. The heart of the DOM is a node tree! By starting at the root of a node tree, programmers can move to other elements by following the parent/child relationships.

The node tree is also used in CSS rules. You have already used nodes without even knowing it. CSS rules rely on being able to select elements and classes so those elements and classes can be styled. The selector part of your rule uses the node tree to figure out what elements to select for the rule.

Look at the selector parts of these two rules:

```
h1 {
    color: #000000;
    font-size: 1.7em;
}

article h1{
    margin: 0;
    padding: 0;
    color: #FFFFFF;
}
```

In the first rule, the "h1" selector says to scan the node tree and select all <**h1**> elements. The second rule uses the "article h1" selector, which says to scan the node tree and select all <**h1**> elements that are inside an <**article**> element. You are going to learn some more advanced ways to use the node tree to select elements for your CSS rules in the rest of this chapter.

Work with Me: Drawing a Node Tree

Let's practice drawing a node tree from one of our existing web pages: "dolphins.html".

1. Run Komodo Edit and load the "dolphins.html" web page

2. Scroll down and find the "MainContent"**<div>**. We are going to focus just on this **<div>** and ignore the rest of the page.

3. On a piece of paper, draw the node tree for all HTML elements within the "MainContent" **<div>**. You don't need any fancy pictures; just list the elements and draw lines between them.

Remember that the node tree does not depend on the text content inside elements. You can imagine the "MainContent" **<div>** with all of the text content removed, so the tree is easier to visualize.

```html
<div id="MainContent">
  <h1> </h1>
  <h2> </h2>
  <figure>
      <img >
      <figcaption> </figcaption>
  </figure>
  <p> <strong> </strong> <strong> </strong> <em> </em> <em> </em> </p>

  <article>
    <aside>
       <p> <a> </a></p>
    </aside>
    <h1> </h1>
    <p> <i> </i> </p>
  </article>
</div>
```

You don't have to write this out yourself, it's just a suggestion for a way of looking at existing HTML code to make the parent and child relationships easier to see. The Activity Solutions menu for Chapter 8 contains an example drawing of a node tree for the "dolphins.html" page.

Lesson Two: Parent and Child Selectors

The relationship between elements on a web page is described by a node tree. You can use the node tree to help select elements in your CSS rules.

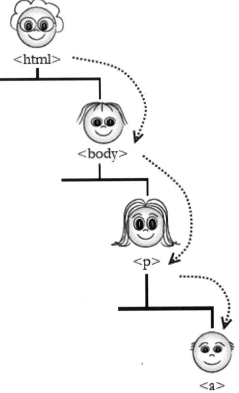

Descendant (Nesting) Selector ("parent child")

A "**descendant**", or "**nesting**" element, is an element that sits inside another element. For example, a link **<a>** might sit inside a paragraph **<p>**, which is inside the **<body>** of the root **<html>** element. The **<a>** element is a child of **<p>**, grandchild of **<body>**, and a great-grandchild of **<html>**. In a node tree children are below their parents, so you "descend" as you move down from parent to child.

The descendant selector will let you apply styles to one element only when it is inside (or a child of) a parent element. To write a descendant selector, write the parent name first, then a space, then the child element.

```
parent child {
    /* These properties will apply to child elements found within parent */
}
```

In your "global.css" file you already have one descendent selector for headlines **<h1>** found inside **<article>** elements. The selector "**article h1**" starts with the parent name "article" and child name "h1" separated by a space.

```
article h1 {
    margin: 0;
    padding: 0;
    color: #FFFFFF;
}
```

Descendent selectors will find child elements nested anywhere inside the parent. So if the **<h1>** element was actually a child of a **<div>** that was inside the **<article>**, the **<h1>** element would still be found by an "article h1" selector.

Multiple Levels ("grandparent parent child")

You can add more relationship levels to a selector if you want to get more specific. You can set the grandparent element in front of the parent for three or more levels like this:

```
grandparent parent child {
    /* These properties will apply to child elements found within parent
       and grandparent */
}
```

Let's think about these two <**div**> elements that each contain a paragraph with a <**strong**> element. One of the <**div**> elements has an **id** equal to "*MainContent*".

```
<div id="MainContent">
  <p>I am inside a <strong>MainContent</strong> div.</p>
</div>
<div>
  <p>I am inside a <strong>regular</strong> div.</p>
</div>
```

Without any styling, both <**strong**> elements appear with the default styles.

> I am inside a **MainContent** div.
>
> I am inside a **regular** div.

Now, let's add a style rule that will apply only to the <**strong**> element inside a <**p**> within the "MainContent" <**div**>.

```
#MainContent p strong {
    font-size:24px;
}
```

Here we have listed the grandparent, parent, and child element in our selector. Notice that each level can include an element name, id, class, or other type of selector. Our grandparent is the element with the "MainContent" id.

> I am inside a **MainContent** div.
>
> I am inside a **regular** div.

Grandchild Selectors ("grandparent * child")

In rare cases you might want to select elements that are **at least** grandchildren of a parent element. To do this you can use an asterisk "*" between the grandparent and child levels instead of a space.

```css
#MainContent * strong {
    font-size:24px;
}
```

With this example we will select <**strong**> elements that are grandchildren (or later) of "#MainContent".

```html
<div id="MainContent">
  <p>I am inside a <strong>paragraph</strong>.</p>
  I am not inside a <strong>paragraph</strong>.
</div>
```

I am inside a **paragraph**.

I am not inside a **paragraph**.

Our rule will apply to the first <**strong**> because it is a grandchild of the "MainContent" element (with <**p**> as a parent). But the second <**strong**> is a direct child of "MainContent" so is not selected.

Direct Child Selectors ("parent > child")

You may want to select a child element only if it is a **direct** child of a parent. You can do this by replacing the space between the parent and child names with a greater than ">" sign like this:

```css
#MainContent > strong {
    font-size:24px;
}
```

I am inside a **paragraph**.

I am not inside a **paragraph**.

Now, with the same HTML code as in the last example, you can see that the <**strong**> element that is directly inside the "MainContent" <**div**> is styled and the <**strong**> element inside a paragraph is not affected, because it is a grandchild.

Combinations of Relationships

It is possible to combine a mixture of selector types such as descendant and direct child by using both spaces and other symbols like ">" in your selector. This example will select all <**strong**> elements that are direct children of a paragraph <**p**> that is found anywhere nested inside a "MainContent" element.

```css
#MainContent p>strong
```

Work with Me: The Emperor Penguin

In this activity we are going to use some parent-child selectors to style a new page about the Emperor Penguin. Because we want to start without many of the styles we have built up for the other pages, we will use a new CSS file called "penguin.css" instead of putting the new rules in our main "global.css".

1. Using Windows Explorer or Mac OS Finder, copy the "penguin.html" file from your "Activity Starters/Chapter08" directory to your "MyProjects/Aquamaniacs" folder.

2. Also copy the "penguin.css" file from your "Activity Starters/Chapter08/SiteStyle" folder to your "MyProjects/Aquamaniacs/SiteStyle" folder.

3. Load the "penguin.html" file on your web browser to see the default styling.

Emperor Penguin

The *Emperor Penguin, a flightless bird*, is the **largest penguin in the world.**

Appearance
The Emperor Penguin has a jet black head, grayish-black wings and back, and a white belly which is why it is often portrayed in comics wearing a **tuxedo.**

Habitat
It lives in the **Antarctic,** a very cold climate, and gives birth to its young during the darkest and coldest time of the year.

Survival
The Emperor Penguin's body has a **triple layer** of dense, oily and waterproof feathers and a thick layer of blubber under the skin to keep it warm in the frigid climate.

Special Skill
With **agility and speed**, the Emperor Penguin can dive to a depth of more than 1,500 ft (450 m) using its small, rigid wings to glide its streamlined body through the water as if it was flying.

Super Dads

Male penguins *huddle* with other males in a huge circle while incubating the eggs.

Males take turns moving from the outer, colder area of the huddle to the inner, warmer area so they all can stay warm.

Eggs are protected in the Male's brood pouch while the female leaves to hunt for food

The male goes without food for nearly *2 months* while the female is away hunting

The "penguin.html" page contains a "PenguinContent" **div** inside the "MainContent" area. Inside the "PenguinContent" **div** are the following elements (with the text removed for clarity):

```
<div id="MainContent">
  <div id="PenguinContent">
    <div>
        <h1> </h1>
    </div>


    <p> <em></em> <i></i> <b></b> </p>


    <div>
      <p> <em></em> <strong></strong> </p>
      <p> <em></em> <strong></strong> </p>
      <p> <em></em> <strong></strong> </p>
      <p> <em></em> <strong></strong> </p>


      <div>
        <h1> </h1>
        <p> <em></em> <i></i> </p>
        <p> <em></em> </p>
        <p> <em></em> </p>
        <p> <em></em> <i></i> </p>
      </div>
    </div>


  </div><!-- end of PenguinContent -->
</div><!-- end of MainContent -->
```

You won't have to make any changes to "penguin.html", but it's good to understand the element relationships in the HTML code so you can write good CSS rules in your "penguin.css" file.

4. Open "penguin.css" in Komodo Edit and scroll down to the very bottom. After the last rule, add the following two new rules to arrange the paragraphs into columns:

```
/* End of starting CSS rules */


#PenguinContent div {
    width: 100%;
    clear: both;
}
```

```
#PenguinContent div p {
    width: 180px;
    margin-right: 20px;
    float: left;
    font-size: 13px;
}
```

The first rule selects all **<div>** elements inside "PenguinContent", and ensures those elements start on their own line by clearing any "float" settings from parent elements. We also set the width to 100% so the **<div>** will cover all available area.

The second rule selects all **<p>** elements inside a **<div>** that belongs to "PenguinContent". For these paragraphs we are setting a fixed width, margin, and font size. We also float the elements to the left so they will appear side-by-side on the page (depending on the width of the browser window).

5. Save your "penguin.css" changes and reload "penguin.html" in your web browser to see the results. The paragraphs within each **<div>** should form small side-by-side columns, and the second **<div>** starts on its own line just like the first **<div>**.

Emperor Penguin

The *Emperor Penguin, a flightless bird*, is the **largest penguin in the world.**

Appearance
The Emperor Penguin has a jet black head, grayish-black wings and back, and a white belly which is why it is often portrayed in comics wearing a **tuxedo.**

Habitat
It lives in the **Antarctic**, a very cold climate, and gives birth to its young during the darkest and coldest time of the year.

Survival
The Emperor Penguin's body has a **triple layer** of dense, oily and waterproof feathers and a thick layer of blubber under the skin to keep it warm in the frigid climate.

Special Skill
With **agility and speed,** the Emperor Penguin can dive to a depth of more than 1,500 ft (450 m) using its small, rigid wings to glide its streamlined body through the water as if it was flying.

Super Dads

Male penguins *huddle* with other males in a huge circle while incubating the eggs.

Males take turns moving from the outer, colder area of the huddle to the inner, warmer area so they all can stay warm.

Eggs are protected in the Male's brood pouch while the female leaves to hunt for food

The male goes without food for nearly 2 months while the female is away hunting

You may have to make your browser window very wide so all 4 columns will appear side-by-side.

6. Finally, let's style the headline elements **<h1>** that are direct children of some **<div>** within "PenguinContent". Add this style rule to the very end of "penguin.css":

```
#PenguinContent div > h1 {
    color: purple;
    font-size: 30px;
}
```

7. Save your "penguin.css" changes and reload "penguin.html" in your web browser. You should see both headlines change to use large purple text.

Emperor Penguin

The *Emperor Penguin, a flightless bird*, is the **largest penguin in the world.**

Super Dads

Notice we used a combination of spaces (descendant) and ">" (direct child) between the parts of our selector. This means we are selecting any element we can find inside the first part ("PenguinContent") that meets the condition of the second part (a direct **<h1>** child of a **<div>**).

Lesson Three: Sibling Selectors

Now that you are comfortable with parent-child selectors, let's turn our attention to "sibling" selectors. A "sibling" is a brother or sister. In terms of a node tree, sibling elements are two or more child elements that share the same parent. This diagram from Lesson One shows several sets of siblings.

On the second row the **<h1>**, **<p>**, and **<p>** elements are siblings and children of the root **<div>**. On the third row there are two different sets of siblings, one belonging to the middle **<p>** and one belonging to the last **<p>**.

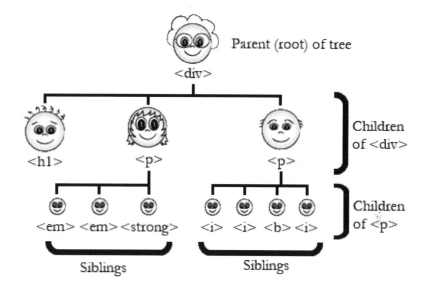

We can use a sibling relationship to select elements for our CSS rules, similar to the way we used parent and child relationships in the last lesson.

Adjacent Sibling Selector ("child + child")

This selector identifies a sibling element that is placed **immediately after** the first sibling element. Both elements need to be children of the **same parent**. To use this selector, place a plus sign "+" between the first sibling and the second sibling in the selector.

To demonstrate sibling selectors, we'll use the following HTML code:

```
<div id="MainContent">
  <p>I am a first sibling paragraph.</p>
  <div>I am a second sibling div.</div>
  <p>I am a third sibling paragraph.</p>
  <p>I am a fourth sibling paragraph.</p>
</div>
```

I am a first sibling paragraph.

I am a second sibling div.

I am a third sibling paragraph.

I am fourth sibling paragraph.

Now, we can add some style rules to start selecting siblings based on their relationship to other siblings in that same parent "MainContent" **<div>**.

The following two CSS rules use adjacent sibling selectors. The first one will select all paragraphs <**p**> that come directly after a <**div**> and make the text content bold. The second rule will select all paragraphs <**p**> that come directly after another <**p**> and turn the text into small caps.

```
div + p {
    font-weight: bold;
}
p + p {
    font-variant: small-caps;
}
```

I am a first sibling paragraph.

I am a second sibling div.

I am a third sibling paragraph.

I AM FOURTH SIBLING PARAGRAPH.

As you can see, the third paragraph becomes bold because it is the only <**p**> element that comes directly after a <**div**> sibling. The fourth paragraph is the only <**p**> element in small caps because it comes directly after another <**p**> sibling.

Distant Sibling Selector ("child ~ child")

The last sibling selector you will learn about is the "distant" sibling selector. This selector will pick a sibling element that comes **anywhere** after the first sibling named in the selector. Remember that "adjacent" selectors only pick elements that are **directly** after the first sibling, but "distant" selectors will find the second element **anywhere** later in the list of siblings for the same parent. The symbol for the distant sibling selector is the tilde (~).

OK, what happens if we change our example to use distant selectors instead of adjacent?

```
div ~ p {
    font-weight: bold;
}
p ~ p {
    font-variant: small-caps;
}
```

I am a first sibling paragraph.

I am a second sibling div.

I AM A THIRD SIBLING PARAGRAPH.

I AM FOURTH SIBLING PARAGRAPH.

The first rule will find any paragraph after a <**div**> sibling, so both of the last two paragraphs are selected for bold text. The second rule will apply to any paragraph found after another paragraph, and both the last two paragraphs come after some <**p**>. So the last two elements are selected for small caps as well.

Remember that "siblings" must be on the same level of the node tree, meaning they belong to the same parent element.

Work with Me: Distant Siblings on the Penguins Page

In this activity you are going to add a distant sibling selector to the Emperor Penguins page.

1. Open your "penguin.css" file in Komodo Edit and scroll down to the very bottom.
2. Add the following rule:

```
#PenguinContent h1 ~ p {
    color: blue;
}
```

This rule should find all paragraphs <p> anywhere after a <h1> sibling element with the "PenguinContent" element. Those selected paragraphs will turn blue in color.

3. Save your changes to "penguin.css" and reload the "penguin.html" file in your browser to check the results. The bottom four paragraphs should be blue because they have a <h1> sibling in the front. But the first four paragraphs do not have a <h1> sibling in front, so they are not changed.

Emperor Penguin

The *Emperor Penguin, a flightless bird,* is the **largest penguin in the world.**

Appearance
The Emperor Penguin has a jet black head, grayish-black wings and back, and a white belly which is why it is often portrayed in comics wearing a **tuxedo.**

Habitat
It lives in the **Antarctic,** a very cold climate, and gives birth to its young during the darkest and coldest time of the year.

Survival
The Emperor Penguin's body has a **triple layer** of dense, oily and waterproof feathers and a thick layer of blubber under the skin to keep it warm in the frigid climate.

Special Skill
With **agility and speed,** the Emperor Penguin can dive to a depth of more than 1,500 ft (450 m) using its small, rigid wings to glide its streamlined body through the water as if it was flying.

Super Dads

Male penguins huddle with other males in a huge circle while incubating the eggs.

Males take turns moving from the outer, colder area of the huddle to the inner, warmer area so they all can stay warm.

Eggs are protected in the Male's brood pouch while the female leaves to hunt for food

The male goes without food for nearly *2 months* while the female is away hunting

Chapter Review

- On a web page a parent element is "built" from a combination of child elements.

- You can apply CSS rules against specific elements based on their relationships in the overall page.

- The Document Object Model or DOM is a common way that web browsers will make the contents of a web page available to programming languages like JavaScript.

- The heart of the DOM is a **node tree** that describes the relationship between elements on a page.

- A "**descendant**", or "**nesting**" element, is an element that sits anywhere inside another element.

- To write a descendant selector, write the parent name first, then a space, then the child element.

- To select elements that are **at least** grandchildren of a parent element, use an asterisk "*" between the grandparent and child levels instead of a space.

- To select a child element only if it is a **direct** child of a parent, replace the space between the parent and child names with a greater than ">" sign.

- It is possible to combine a mixture of selector types such as descendant and direct child by using both spaces and other symbols like ">" in your selector.

- To select a sibling element that is placed **immediately after** the first sibling element with the same parent, place a plus sign "+" between the first sibling and the second sibling in the selector.

- The "distant" sibling selector will pick a sibling element that comes **anywhere** after the first sibling named in the selector, using a tilde (~) between siblings.

Your Turn Activity: Emperor Penguins

In this activity you are going to finish your new "Emperor Penguins" page by adding several more style rules with relational selectors.

Your activity requirements and instructions are found in the "Chapter_08_Activity.pdf" document located in your "KidCoder/AdvancedWebDesign/Activity Docs" folder. You can access this document through your Student Menu or by double-clicking on it from Windows Explorer or Mac OS Finder.

Complete this activity now and ensure you understand the material before continuing!

Chapter Nine: Pseudo-Selectors

So far you have written CSS rules with selectors based on an element's name, class, id, or relationship to other elements. In this chapter you will learn about "pseudo-selectors", which are selectors that pick elements or parts of elements based on other conditions.

Lesson One: Pseudo-Class and Pseudo-Element Selectors

The word "**pseudo**" means "fake" or "having an appearance of". "**Pseudo-selectors**" are not full selectors themselves, but are used to modify other selectors. Pseudo-selectors will add style to an element **when it meets a condition**. Pseudo-selectors can also style **part** of an element such as the first line or the first letter in a paragraph.

Pseudo-selectors are added to some base selector such as the element name, class, or id. After the base part you add a colon ":" and then the pseudo-selector name. Do not put any spaces between the selector, colon or pseudo-selector.

```
selector:pseudo-class {
}
selector:pseudo-element {
}
```

All pseudo-selectors fall into one of two groups: "**pseudo-class**" or "**pseudo-element**". It's really hard to tell the difference between the groups, so we'll just call them all pseudo-selectors.

The Hover State Pseudo-selectors

Hover states allow you to change styles on an element when the user interacts with it using the mouse. You have already used the ":link", ":visited", ":hover", and ":active" selectors on <a> hyperlinks. CSS3 allows us to use these hover states on any element in your node tree. The ":visited" state has become somewhat discouraged for security reasons because it gives a visible trace of places you have already visited. So you can still style that state, but it may be best to make visited links look the same as default links.

Notice that the hover state pseudo-selectors follow the correct pattern with the element selector first, then a colon, then the pseudo-selector, and no space in-between.

```
a:link {
}
a:visited {
}
a:hover {
}
a:active {
}
```

You used these hover state selectors earlier for annotating figures. Instead of styling hyperlinks, you styled list items <**li**> by making text visible when the mouse hovered over the item.

```
.annotated li:hover
{
    background-color: white;
    text-indent: 0px;
    cursor: default;
}
```

Notice this selector uses the parent-child relationship also, selecting only list items that are nested children of an "annotated" class element when the mouse is hovering over the item.

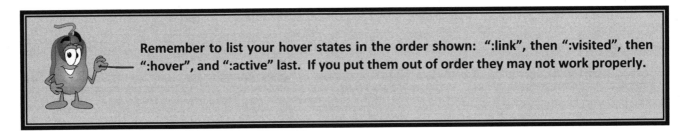

Remember to list your hover states in the order shown: ":link", then ":visited", then ":hover", and ":active" last. If you put them out of order they may not work properly.

First Letter Pseudo-selectors (":first-letter")

You can use the "**:first-letter**" pseudo-selector to style the first letter of an element. This will only work on block-level elements like paragraphs, headlines, or <**div**>, so don't try to apply them to inline elements such as <**em**> or <**strong**>.

Let's try out an example! Here is a tongue-twisting paragraph:

```
<p>Peter Piper picked a peck of pickled peppers.  A peck of pickled peppers
Peter Piper picked.  If Peter Piper picked a peck of pickled peppers, where's
the peck of pickled peppers that Peter Piper picked?</p>
```

OK, now let's style the first letter of all paragraphs to give it a large, bold look:

```
p:first-letter {
    font-weight: bold;
    font-size: 24px;
}
```

Now we can see that only the first letter in the paragraph has the new style:

Peter Piper picked a peck of pickled peppers. A peck of pickled peppers
Peter Piper picked. If Peter Piper picked a peck of pickled peppers, where's
the peck of pickled peppers that Peter Piper picked?

The First Line Pseudo-selector (":first-line")

The ":first-line" pseudo-selector works the same way as ":first-letter", except the style is applied to the entire first line of an element. Again, this will only work for block-level elements. Let's switch our CSS rule to use ":first-line" instead of ":first-letter".

```
p:first-line {
    font-weight: bold;
    font-size: 24px;
}
```

Peter Piper picked a peck of pickled peppers.
A peck of pickled peppers Peter Piper picked. If Peter Piper picked a peck of
pickled peppers, where's the peck of pickled peppers that Peter Piper picked?

The browser will automatically adjust the style to stay on just the first line as the size of the browser window changes.

Peter Piper picked a peck of pickled
peppers. A peck of pickled peppers Peter Piper picked. If
Peter Piper picked a peck of pickled peppers, where's the
peck of pickled peppers that Peter Piper picked?

Work with Me: Playing with ":first-letter" and ":first-line"

We are going to experiment with all pseudo-selectors in this chapter using an HTML page that is not part of the main Aquamaniacs web site.

1. To get started, copy the "Activity Starters/Chapter09/positions.html" page to your "MyProjects/Aquamaniacs" folder. The HTML file can sit in that folder for easy access from your Komodo Edit project, even though none of the Aquamaniacs pages link to it.

2. Load the "Aquamaniacs/positions.html" page in your web browser to see the default content.

Paragraph One: *(First em)* **(bold 1)** *(Second em)* **(bold 2)** *(Third em)* *(Fourth em)*

Div One: *(First em)* *(Second em)* **(bold 1)** *(Third em)* **(bold 1)**

Paragraph Two: *(First em)* **(bold 1)** *(Second em)* *(Third em)* *(Fourth em)* **(bold 2)** *(Fifth em)* *(Sixth em)*

Div Two: *(First em)* *(Second em)* **(bold 1)** *(Third em)* **(bold 2)** *(Fourth em)* **(bold 3)**

3. Now, load the "positions.html" file in Komodo Edit and look at the **<body>** content. You will find a **<p>**, **<div>**, **<p>**, and **<div>** directly under the body, each with a variety of **<em>** and **<b>** elements inside.

4. This page does not link to "global.css" or any Aquamaniacs styles! Because it's a simple test page we will put all of our pseudo-selector styles embedded in the **<head>** area. Scroll up and find the existing **<style>** section with coloring and padding for the **<em>** and **<b>** elements.

5. Add a new rule in between the commented line and the closing **</style>** tag as shown below. This rule should change the first letter of every **<p>** to a larger bold size with yellow background.

```
/* new experimental styles should go below */
p:first-letter {
    background-color: yellow;
    font-weight: bold;
    font-size: 20px;
}
</style>
```

6. Save your changes to "positions.html" and reload it in a browser to see the effects. Do you see the first letter change as shown below?

Paragraph One: *(First em)* **(bold 1)** *(Second em)* **(bold 2)** *(Third em)* *(Fourth em)*

Div One: *(First em)* *(Second em)* **(bold 1)** *(Third em)* **(bold 1)**

Paragraph Two: *(First em)* **(bold 1)** *(Second em)* *(Third em)* *(Fourth em)* **(bold 2)** *(Fifth em)* *(Sixth em)*

Div Two: *(First em)* *(Second em)* **(bold 1)** *(Third em)* **(bold 2)** *(Fourth em)* **(bold 3)**

7. Go back to the **\<style\>** area and change your CSS rule to a different selector to pick the first line of every **\<div\>**.

```
/* new experimental styles should go below */
p:first-letter div:first-line {
    background-color: yellow;
    font-weight: bold;
    font-size: 20px;
}
</style>
```

Paragraph One: *(First em)* **(bold 1)** *(Second em)* **(bold 2)** *(Third em)* *(Fourth em)*

Div One: ***(First em)*** ***(Second em)*** **(bold 1)** ***(Third em)*** **(bold 1)**

Paragraph Two: *(First em)* **(bold 1)** *(Second em)* *(Third em)* *(Fourth em)* **(bold 2)** *(Fifth em)* *(Sixth em)*

Div Two: ***(First em)*** ***(Second em)*** **(bold 1)** ***(Third em)*** **(bold 2)** ***(Fourth em)*** **(bold 3)**

8. Now make your web browser window smaller and watch how only the first line of each **\<div\>** shows the new style. Any text that wraps to the next line will not be changed.

Paragraph One: *(First em)* **(bold 1)** *(Second em)* **(bold 2)** *(Third em)* *(Fourth em)*

Div One: ***(First em)*** ***(Second em)*** **(bold 1)** ***(Third em)*** (bold 1)

Paragraph Two: *(First em)* **(bold 1)** *(Second em)* *(Third em)* *(Fourth em)* **(bold 2)** *(Fifth em)* *(Sixth em)*

Div Two: ***(First em)*** ***(Second em)*** **(bold 1)** ***(Third em)*** **(bold 2)** *(Fourth em)* **(bold 3)**

Lesson Two: First and Last Child Pseudo-Selectors

In this quick lesson you are going to learn how to select the first or last child of any parent. We'll use this HTML code with four paragraphs in a **<div>** with some **<em>** and **<strong>** styles for our examples:

```
<div>
  <p><strong>Jack</strong>, be <strong>nimble</strong>,</p>
  <p><em>Jack</em>, be <em>quick</em>,</p>
  <p><strong>Jack</strong>, jump <em>over</em></p>
  <p>the candlestick.</p>
</div>
```

Jack, be **nimble**,

Jack, be *quick*,

Jack, jump *over*

the candlestick.

The First Child Pseudo-Selector (":first-child")

The ":first-child" pseudo-selector will select the target element only if it is the **first** child of the parent element. If we apply it to paragraphs **<p>** in our example, it will select the first paragraph because it is the first child of the parent **<div>**.

```
p:first-child {
    background-color: yellow;
}
```

Jack, be **nimble**,

Jack, be *quick*,

Jack, jump *over*

the candlestick.

Jack, be **nimble**,

Jack, be *quick*,

Jack, jump *over*

the candlestick.

Let's switch the ":first-child" to both **<strong>** and **<em>** elements. Now the first **<strong>** and **<em>** element inside any parent are selected.

```
strong:first-child, em:first-child {
    background-color: yellow;
}
```

The Last Child Pseudo-Selector (":last-child")

The ":last-child" pseudo-selector works exactly like ":first-child", except it will select elements that are the **last** child of a parent. We'll just change our last examples to use ":last-child" and see the expected results.

```
p:last-child {
    background-color: yellow;
}
```

Jack, be **nimble**,

Jack, be *quick*,

Jack, jump *over*

the candlestick.

Jack, be **nimble**,

Jack, be *quick*,

Jack, jump *over*

the candlestick.

```
strong:last-child, em:last-child {
    background-color: yellow;
}
```

The last paragraph and the last **<strong>** and **<em>** elements have been selected in each case.

Work with Me: Playing with ":first-child" and ":last-child"

Let's continue with our simple "positions.html" page from the last lesson to experiment with the ":first-child" and ":last-child" pseudo-selectors.

1. Load your "Aquamaniacs/positions.html" page into Komodo Edit.
2. Change the bottom style rule that you added to select the **<em>** element where it is a first child.

```
/* new experimental styles should go below */
div:first-line em:first-child {
    background-color: yellow;
    font-weight: bold;
    font-size: 20px;
}
```

3. Save your changes and load "positions.html" into a web browser to see the results. The first child in both **<p>** and **<div>** elements happens to be an **<em>**, so all four first children are selected.

Paragraph One: *(First em)* (bold 1) *(Second em)* (bold 2) *(Third em)* *(Fourth em)*

Div One: *(First em)* *(Second em)* (bold 1) *(Third em)* (bold 1)

Paragraph Two: *(First em)* (bold 1) *(Second em)* *(Third em)* *(Fourth em)* (bold 2) *(Fifth em)* *(Sixth em)*

Div Two: *(First em)* *(Second em)* (bold 1) *(Third em)* (bold 2) *(Fourth em)* (bold 3)

4. Now change your rule to select the **<b>** element where it is the last child.

```
/* new experimental styles should go below */
em:first-child b:last-child {
    background-color: yellow;
    font-weight: bold;
    font-size: 20px;
}
```

5. Save your changes and reload "positions.html". Can you guess what elements will be styled?

Paragraph One: *(First em)* (bold 1) *(Second em)* (bold 2) *(Third em)* *(Fourth em)*

Div One: *(First em)* *(Second em)* (bold 1) *(Third em)* **(bold 1)**

Paragraph Two: *(First em)* (bold 1) *(Second em)* *(Third em)* *(Fourth em)* (bold 2) *(Fifth em)* *(Sixth em)*

Div Two: *(First em)* *(Second em)* (bold 1) *(Third em)* (bold 2) *(Fourth em)* **(bold 3)**

You guessed it; the last child in each **<div>** is a **<b>**, so only those two elements are selected.

Lesson Three: Numbered and Combined Selectors

Web browsers will assign position numbers to each node in a node tree. Numbers start at 1 and go up by 1 for each sibling further down in the HTML file. Each time the browser reaches a new child level within the tree, numbering starts over with 1 for the first child. When the browser reaches the last child for a parent, counting stops for that set of siblings. The example tree below shows the numbers that would be assigned to each node.

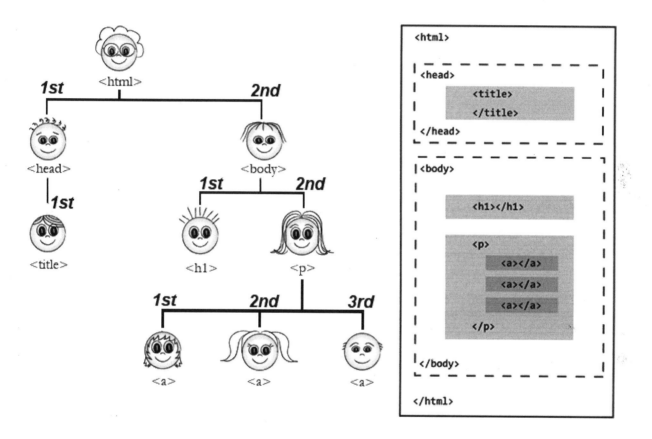

We can use pseudo-selectors and these node numbers to select the first, second, third, fourth, or other elements within a parent.

The nth-child() Pseudo-selector (":nth-child(n)")

The ":nth-child(n)" pseudo-selector will match every element that is the nth child of its parent. For example, this rule will select every **<strong>** element that is the second child of a parent.

```
strong:nth-child(2) {
    background-color: yellow;
}
```

We can apply this rule to the same example HTML from the last lesson.

```
<div>
    <p><strong>Jack</strong>, be <strong>nimble</strong>,</p>
    <p><em>Jack</em>, be <em>quick</em>,</p>
    <p><strong>Jack</strong>, jump <em>over</em></p>
    <p>the candlestick.</p>
</div>
```

Jack, be nimble,

Jack, be quick,

Jack, jump over

the candlestick.

Jack, be **nimble**,

Jack, be quick,

Jack, jump over

the candlestick.

As you can see, the second **<strong>** element in the first paragraph was selected. No other elements are selected in other parents because there is no other **<strong>** element that is in position 2 when counting all of the children. It's easy to create a rule that does not select any elements. If your number is too high, then no parent may have that many children.

Instead of a number, you can use one of the keywords "**odd**" or "**even**" to select every odd or even child. Let's change our example to use out the "odd" keyword.

```
strong:nth-child(odd) {
    background-color: yellow;
}
```

Jack, be nimble,

Jack, be quick,

Jack, jump over

the candlestick.

Now we have selected every odd **<strong>** element (1st, 3rd, 5th, etc.). In our HTML code the 1st **<strong>** element will be selected, but we don't have any at higher odd numbers.

The nth-of-type() Pseudo-selector (":nth-of-type(n)")

The ":nth-of-type(n)" selector works much like the ":nth-child" selector, except it will count only elements of the target type. Any other elements of different types are completely ignored for counting as if they were not present at all. This example will select the first **<em>** of any parent, even if other types of elements come beforehand in the node tree.

```
em:nth-of-type(1) {
    background-color: yellow;
}
```

Jack, be **nimble**,

Jack, be quick,

Jack, jump over

the candlestick.

Notice that the first **<em>** in both paragraphs is selected, even though the **<em>** in the second paragraph is actually the second child in the tree. The first **<strong>** child is ignored when counting, so the **<em>** with "over" is the first child of the target type.

Work with Me: Playing with Numbered Selectors

Now let's work with our simple "positions.html" page to experiment with the ":nth-child" and ":nth-of-type" pseudo-selectors.

1. Load your "Aquamaniacs/positions.html" page into Komodo Edit.

2. Change the bottom style rule that you added to select the <**em**> elements that are the third child.

```
/* new experimental styles should go below */
b:last-child em:nth-child(3) {
  background-color: yellow;
  font-weight: bold;
  font-size: 20px;
}
```

3. Save your changes and load "positions.html" into a web browser to see the results. The <**em**> elements that are in the 3rd child position should be selected. As you can see, the <**em**> elements containing "(Second em)" in the first and second paragraphs are the third children in each case.

Paragraph One: *(First em)* **(bold 1)** *(Second em)* **(bold 2)** *(Third em)* *(Fourth em)*

Div One: *(First em)* *(Second em)* **(bold 1)** *(Third em)* **(bold 1)**

Paragraph Two: *(First em)* **(bold 1)** *(Second em)* *(Third em)* *(Fourth em)* **(bold 2)** *(Fifth em)* *(Sixth em)*

Div Two: *(First em)* *(Second em)* **(bold 1)** *(Third em)* **(bold 2)** *(Fourth em)* **(bold 3)**

4. Now change your rule to select the third <**em**> element of that type.

```
/* new experimental styles should go below */
em:nth-child(3) em:nth-of-type(3) {
  background-color: yellow;
  font-weight: bold;
  font-size: 20px;
}
```

5. Save your changes and reload "positions.html". Can you guess what elements will be styled?

Paragraph One: *(First em)* **(bold 1)** *(Second em)* **(bold 2)** *(Third em)* *(Fourth em)*

Div One: *(First em)* *(Second em)* **(bold 1)** *(Third em)* **(bold 1)**

Paragraph Two: *(First em)* **(bold 1)** *(Second em)* *(Third em)* *(Fourth em)* **(bold 2)** *(Fifth em)* *(Sixth em)*

Div Two: *(First em)* *(Second em)* **(bold 1)** *(Third em)* **(bold 2)** *(Fourth em)* **(bold 3)**

We have picked the third <em> element in each parent by counting only the <em> child elements.

Combining Pseudo-selectors

What if you want to do something that requires both relational and pseudo-selectors such as picking the first child from a specific parent? CSS has made that task easy by allowing you to combine pseudo-selectors with descendant relationships. You can select the element by using one of the relationships from the last lesson (space, *, >, +, ~) and then apply a pseudo-selector to the results (":first-child", ":last-child", etc.). Combining pseudo-selectors with relational selectors can result in some really neat effects.

In this example we select <em> elements that are nested children of a <p>, and then further select only those elements that are the first child of the parent.

Jack, be **nimble**,

Jack, be *quick*,

Jack, jump *over*

the candlestick.

```
p em:first-child {
    background-color: yellow;
}
```

Here is a more complicated example. We start by selecting all <p> that are direct children of a <div> ("div>p"). Then we take those <p> that are the 3rd child of the parent ("p>nth-child(3)"). Finally we add a space for a nested selector and find all <em> elements that are the last child of the parent ("em:last-child").

Jack, be **nimble**,

Jack, be *quick*,

Jack, jump *over*

the candlestick.

```
div>p:nth-child(3) em:last-child {
    background-color: yellow;
}
```

As a result, we have selected the last <em> in the 3rd paragraph belonging to the parent <div>. These combined selectors can be tricky to understand, but are very powerful when you need them. Many times, it is easier to just put an **id** or **class** on an element and style the **class** or **id** directly instead of figuring out complicated relationships. Pseudo-selectors and descendant relationships play a large role when you start designing animated navigation bars and using JavaScript and jQuery.

Work with Me: Adding a Drop-Cap Effect

Have you seen documents that have a "drop-cap" on the first letter of every paragraph? A drop-cap is a much larger letter at the very start of the paragraph that drops down several lines. You can use drop-caps to add a little extra style to your page. We are going to create this effect using a combination of relational selectors and the ":first-letter" pseudo-selector.

1. Open your "global.css" file in Komodo Edit
2. Scroll down to the bottom and add the following style rule that will select only the first letter of paragraphs that are direct children of a "MainContent" element.

```
#MainContent>p:first-letter {
    font-size: 100px;
    color: #717B32;
    float: left;
    padding: 0;
    margin: 0px 5px 5px 0px;
    line-height: 65px;
    text-shadow: 3px 3px 7px black;
}
```

3. Save your changes and load both "index.html" and "dolphins.html" in your web browser. Both of these pages have a paragraph as a direct child of "MainContent". You should see a drop-cap effect on the first letters "O" and "F" of both child paragraphs inside "MainContent".

WELCOME TO AQUAMANIACS

Our oceans hold many wild and wonderful sea creatures. Here, you can learn about large animals like whales, dolphins, and sharks. See oddities like the sea urchin, longhorn cowfish, emperor penguin, lobster, lionfish, cuttlefish, and seahorse. Don't forget to visit the octopus and otter!

Similarly, the first paragraph on the Dolphins page also now has the large drop-cap letter.

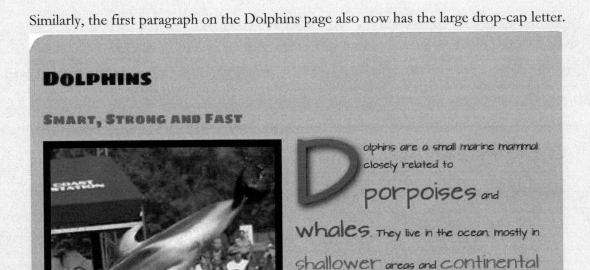

You may find on a page with many paragraphs that the drop-cap effect can look too busy or distracting. You might want to pick another way to style selected letters using **<span>** elements with a specific class or other more complicated rules using relationships and pseudo-selectors.

Chapter Review

- "**Pseudo-selectors**" are not full selectors themselves, but are used to modify other selectors.
- Pseudo-selectors will add style to an element **when it meets a condition**.
- All pseudo-selectors fall into one of two groups: "**pseudo-class**" or "**pseudo-element**".
- CSS3 allows us to use hover states on any element in your node tree.
- If you list the hover states out of a specific order, they may not work properly.
- You can use the "**:first-letter**" pseudo-selector to style the first letter of an element.
- The "**:first-line**" pseudo-selector styles the entire first line of an element.
- The "**:first-child**" pseudo-selector will select the target element only if it is the **first** child.
- The "**:last-child**" pseudo-selector will select elements that are the **last** child of a parent.
- The "**:nth-child(n)**" pseudo-selector will match every element that is the nth child of its parent.
- Instead of a number, you can use one of the keywords "**odd**" or "**even**" in the **nth-child** pseudo-selector to select every odd or even child.
- The "**:nth-of-type(n)**" selector will count only elements of the target type.
- CSS allows you to combine pseudo-selectors with descendant relationships.
- Combining pseudo-selectors with relational selectors can result in some really neat effects.
- Pseudo-selectors and descendant relationships play a large role when you start designing animated navigation bars and using JavaScript and jQuery.

Your Turn Activity: Lobsters

In this activity you are going to create a new "Lobsters" page to show off your new pseudo-selector skills.

Your activity requirements and instructions are found in the "Chapter_09_Activity.pdf" document located in your "KidCoder/AdvancedWebDesign/Activity Docs" folder. You can access this document through your Student Menu or by double-clicking on it from Windows Explorer or Mac OS Finder.

Complete this activity now and ensure you understand the material before continuing!

Chapter Ten: Dynamic Menus

Have you ever seen a website with a fancy drop-down menu system? These menus show expanded navigation links as you hover a mouse over a category topic. You are going to learn how to create these dynamic menus yourself using CSS.

Lesson One: Dynamic Menus and Nested Lists

When your web site becomes large, it is hard to put links for every page into one long list. Your Aquamaniacs website so far has kept all of the navigation links in a **<nav>** area to the left of the page. But this sidebar is very long and you have to scroll down to see all the links.

Web designers have created "**drop-down**" or "**dynamic**" menus as a neat alternative to a huge list of links. Drop-down menus start with a single small list of items across the top or side. When you hover your mouse over a topic, more topics pop-out. If the navigation bar is along the top, generally the new list drops down. If the navigation bar is along the side, the new list could pop out to the side or drop the whole menu down to make room for the new links.

AQUAMANIACS

- Home
- Big Critters
    - Whales
    - Dolphins
    - Sharks
- Oddballs
    - Emperor Penguin
    - Lobster
    - Lionfish
    - Cuttlefish
    - Seahorse
- Multimedia

Take a look at the example web page to the left about "My 2 Dogs". This site has a **<nav>** bar at the top with three main topics:

- Home
- Hunter
- Shadow

My 2 Dogs

| HOME | HUNTER | SHADOW |

Welcome to my website about my favorite two dogs: "Hunter" and "Shadow".

Click on the menu above to see details about each pooch!

©2013. Me, Inc. All Rights Reserved.

If you hover your mouse over any topic, it will give you a drop-down list of links relating to that topic.

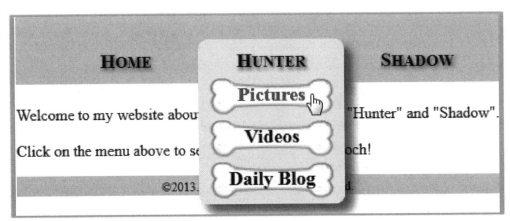

That's pretty neat right? Each drop-down menu has a list of links along with special effects like a background image, rounded corners, shadows, and so on. Fortunately, we can make fancy menus using HTML and CSS skills you have already learned. Dynamic menus can be formed using a combination of lists <li> and CSS styles that use the relationships and pseudo-states we covered in the last couple of chapters.

Nested Lists for Navigation

You can picture a drop-down menu as a set of lists within other lists. That means that each list item <li> itself contains another full list <ul> inside. These "nested" lists form the HTML heart of a drop-down menu. The HTML <nav> area for our example "My 2 Dogs" website looks like this:

```
<nav>
    <ul>
        <li id="home"><a href="index.html">Home</a></li>
        <li><a href="#">Hunter</a>
            <ul>
                <li><a href="">Pictures</a></li>
                <li><a href="">Videos</a></li>
                <li><a href="">Daily Blog</a></li>
            </ul>
        </li>
        <li><a href="#">Shadow</a>
            <ul>
                <li><a href="">Pictures</a></li>
                <li><a href="">Videos</a></li>
                <li><a href="">Diet</a></li>
            </ul>
        </li>
    </ul>
</nav>
```

Notice that inside the <**nav**> area we have one unordered list <**ul**>. This list contains the top-level items "Home", "Hunter", and "Shadow" that appear on the main menu bar. The "Hunter" and "Shadow" list items each also contain another full list <**ul**> with hyperlinks relating to that main topic.

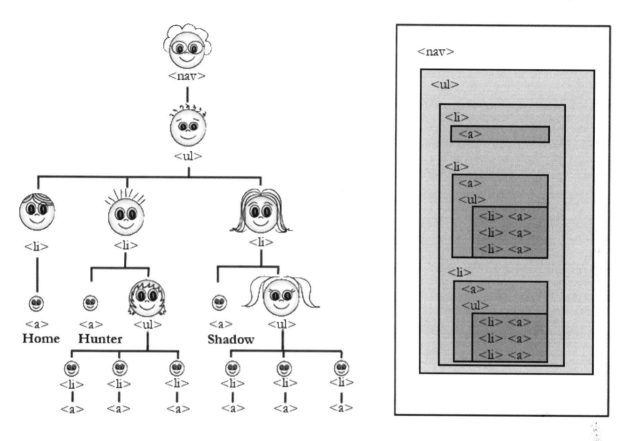

The diagram above shows the node tree and relationships within our example <**nav**> element. It will be very important to understand these relationships because we will be using CSS rules to pick out elements for styling to make the dynamic menu work. Can you tell which nodes actually hold the "Home", "Hunter", and "Shadow" links? We've marked them on the top three <**a**> elements above. The bottom-most six <**a**> elements hold each of the sub-menu links such as "Pictures" or "Videos".

Notice that one of our top-level list items contains a link to the "Home" page, "index.html". The other two top-level list items contain a hyperlink to "#" for the top-level text, plus another list for the sub-topics.

```
<li id="home"><a href="index.html">Home</a></li>
<li><a href="#">Hunter</a>
    <ul>
```

The "#" link means "stay right here" and will not actually take the user anywhere. Our style rules are a bit easier if we make all of the top list items contain hyperlinks, even if they are not intended to be live links.

To build a dynamic menu, you'll be using mostly skills you have already learned, but putting them together in some creative ways that are new to you. Our CSS rules will apply positioning, display, colors, background images, rounded corners, text shadows, and other special effects to build a truly professional-looking menu.

Work with Me: The Aquamaniacs <nav> Node Tree

Making a dynamic menu with CSS requires a careful understanding of your node tree. The Aquamaniacs <nav> section is already present in your HTML pages, but we have not spent much type studying it yet. Let's take a deeper look at the nested list elements you are going to style.

1. Run Komodo Edit and load any of your HTML pages such as "index.html".
2. Scroll down and find the <nav> section. The <nav> contains a set of nested unordered lists, and the first couple of groups are shown below.

```
<nav>
     <ul>
          <!-- first link group -->
          <li id="home"><a href="index.html">Home</a>
          </li>
          <!-- second link group -->
          <li><a href="#">Big Critters</a>
               <ul>
                    <li><a href="whales.html">Whales</a>
                    <li><a href="dolphins.html">Dolphins</a>
                    <li><a href="sharks.html">Sharks</a>
               </ul>
          </li>
```

3. Get a sheet of paper and pencil, and draw the node tree for the Aquamaniacs <nav> section. You don't need to make cute pictures for each node, but label the nodes so you understand what is inside. Use the example given earlier in the lesson as a guide and pattern to follow.

Styling the Aquamaniacs Header

Right now our Aquamaniacs **<header>** area contains a plain **<div>**, a **<h1>**, and our **<nav>** bar to the side. We need to make some improvements to our header to get ready for dynamic menus.

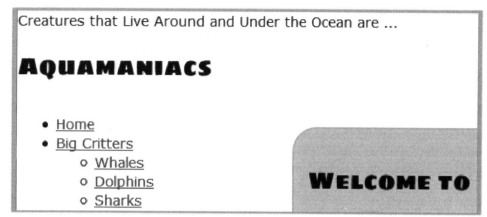

In the next Work with Me, you are going to:

- Style the header and **<h1>** with a fancy background image
- Add a background gradient and other styling to the top tag line **<div>**
- Remove the **<nav>** settings making it float to the left, so it will appear on top of the MainContent
- Change the MainContent area to work better with the menu on top

Work with Me: Preparing the Aquamaniacs Header

Let's take some steps to prepare the Aquamaniacs Header for the new dynamic menus we'll create later in the chapter.

1. Using Windows Explorer or Mac OS Finder, copy the following images from your "Activity Starters/Chapter10/SiteStyle" folder to your "MyProjects/Aquamaniacs/SiteStyle" folder:
   - "banner.jpg"
   - "nav-drop.jpg"
   - "nav-gradient.jpg"
2. Open your "global.css" file in Komodo Edit and scroll down just below the existing **<body>** rule. This is where you are going to add new style rules for the header.

175

3. Add the following three rules between the existing **<body>** and **<p>** rules:

```css
header {
    text-align: center;
    margin: 0 0 30px 0;
    background: #BBE1C1 url(banner.jpg) no-repeat center bottom;
    height: 182px;
    padding: 0px;
}
header h1{
    color:#000000;
    font-size: 80px;
    margin: 0;
    padding: 15px 0 23px 0;
}

#tagline {
    color: #FFFFFF;
    font-size: 12px;
    font-weight: bold;
    margin: 0px;
    background: #717B32 url(nav-gradient.png) repeat-x 0px -25px;
    height: 12px;
    padding: 5px;
    line-height: 11px;
    text-shadow: 0 1px 1px rgba(0,0,0,0.3);
}
```

The first rule will center all text in the header and set up a nice background image. The second rule will set the font color, size, margin, and padding for the main headline. The third rule will style just the **<div>** with the "tagline" id at the very top, giving it a background gradient, text shadow, and other small size and padding adjustments.

4. When you are done, save your changes to "global.css" and load "index.html" into your web browser to see the results.

You should see a big difference in your <**header**> area!

5. Next, in "global.css" find your existing style for the <**nav**> element and the "MainContent" <**div**>. Delete the <**nav**> style entirely and make the changes shown below to "MainContent".

```
nav {
    float: left;
    width: 20%;
}

#MainContent {
    float: right left;
    width: 70%;
    margin: 15px 5px 15px 15px 25px 5px 30px 25px;
```

By removing the <**nav**> rule the navigation bar will now appear between the header and the main content, which is where we want it for dynamic menus. With the <**nav**> bar removed from the left-hand side, we can also change the "MainContent" **float** from *right* to *left* and also adjust the margin settings.

6. When done, save your changes to "global.css" and reload "index.html" in your web browser.

Don't panic when you see the results!

The **<nav>** elements now appear on top of the MainContent area due to styles on the parent **<header>**. That's OK, when we turn these into drop-down menus they will neatly fit in the available space. Remember, you have to break some eggs to bake a cake.

Lesson Two: Styling First-Level Dynamic Menus

In this lesson we're going to work on styles for the top level of a dynamic menu. We'll continue using the

"My 2 Dogs" example from the last lesson, and you'll also work with the Aquamaniacs navigation bar.

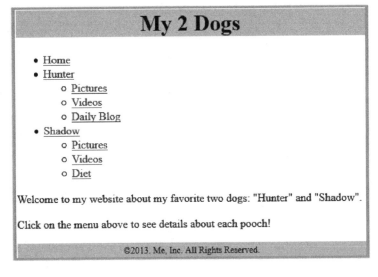

The dynamic menu starts as a simple set of nested list items with hyperlinks. Before any styling, you would see this plain navigation bar (similar to your Aquamaniacs bar).

We have our work cut out for us!

The "display" Property

Dynamic menus will use the **display** property, so let's study this feature before going any further. You know that some elements like <div> and <p> are "block" elements. That means the browser will automatically start them on a new line and add some default spacing around them. Other elements like <strong> or <em> are "inline" elements that do not get any special spacing. You can use the **display** property to change the behavior of an element between inline and block, or even hide the element completely! The following table shows some common **display** properties.

inline	The element will be displayed "inline" without any extra spacing or line breaks.
block	The element will be displayed as a "block" on its own line with extra spacing.
inline-block	The element will be displayed "inline" as a whole, but contents inside the element are treated as a block.
none	The element is hidden completely and does not take up any space in the layout.

To see the display property in action, let's experiment with the two <p> elements on our "My 2 Dogs" main page. Normally these paragraphs are block elements, so each <p> will start on its own line. But when we apply an "*inline*" **display**, the paragraphs run together as inline elements.

```
p {
      display: inline;
}
```

Welcome to my website about my favorite two dogs: "Hunter" and "Shadow". Click on the menu above to see details about each pooch!

©2013. Me, Inc. All Rights Reserved.

We can also change the **display** to "*none*" and the paragraphs will be hidden entirely.

```
p {
    display: none;
}
```

©2013. Me, Inc. All Rights Reserved.

We'll use the "*inline-block*" value on our dynamic menus to arrange groups of items "inline" from left to right across the navigation bar. The elements inside each menu will still be treated as a block. We'll also use the "*none*" value to hide these menu blocks when we don't want to see them.

First CSS Rules for a Dynamic <nav> Menu

Let's begin by adding two style rules for the **<nav>** element and any **<li>** elements inside the **<nav>**.

```css
/* styles for the overall nav area */
nav {
    background-color:lightgray;
    display: inline-block;
    text-align: center;
    margin: 0px;
    padding-top: 8px;
    width: 100%;
}
/* styles for all list items anywhere in the nav area */
nav li {
    width: 150px;
    margin: 0;
    padding: 0 0 8px 0;
    float: left;
    position: relative;
    list-style: none;
    z-index: 10;
}
```

The first **<nav>** rule will change the overall background color, center the text, make the **<nav>** bar stretch the entire width of the page, and set the **display** to *inline-block*. The second rule will select all <li> elements nested anywhere inside the **<nav>** and set a fixed width, margin, and padding. The elements are also floated to the left with relative positioning and set to a high **z-index** to stay on top of other content. Finally, we set the **list-style** to *none* to remove the bullet image from the left side of the item.

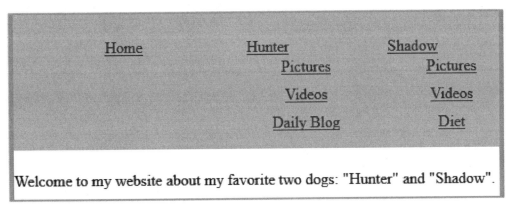

Now, as you can see, our list items are floated from left to right across the top with a light gray background. The list bullets have been removed, and each list element is positioned relative to its parent.

Styling the Hyperlinks

Next we're going to style the hyperlinks <a> to remove the underlines and set our own colors and appearance.

```
/* styles for all hyperlinks within the nav area */
nav a {
    padding: 5px 0px;
    margin: 0;
    font-weight: bold;
    font-size: 20px;
    font-variant: normal;
    color: black;
    display: block;
    text-decoration: none;
}
/* styles for top-level hyperlinks in the top list */
nav>ul>li>a {
    font-variant: small-caps;
    text-shadow: 2px 2px 3px rgba(0,0,0,0.6);
}
```

The first rule applies to all <a> within the <nav>, and it sets some margins and padding as well as making the font larger, bold, and black. We set the **display** to *block* and **text-decoration** to *none* to remove the default underline given to hyperlinks.

The second rule applies just to the top-level hyperlinks using the "direct child" selector ">". We want to select the anchors that are direct children of list items that are direct children of <ul> that itself is a direct child of <nav>. In other words, we picked the top-level <li> but none of the nested <li>. For these top-level hyperlinks, we'll use a small caps effect with a text shadow.

Work with Me: Starting the Aquamaniacs Drop-Down Menus

It's time to get started on the Aquamaniacs drop-down menus! Because we'll be adding a large number of new CSS rules, we'll split them out into a new CSS file called "navigation.css". All of your HTML files already have a <**link**> to this stylesheet, but we haven't used it until now.

1. To begin, run Komodo edit and right-click on your "SiteStyle" folder in the Aquamaniacs project area.

- Select "New File from Template…".
- Select the "Web" category and then the "CSS" Template.
- Type in "navigation.css" as the filename and click "Open".

You should now see a new "navigation.css" file in your project under the SiteStyle folder. When you open it into the center editing area, the file will be blank.

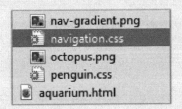

OK, now we can begin to build the CSS rules for our drop-down menu. Some of these rules will be a bit tricky to type out, so if you have any trouble, carefully compare your work to the description. Don't forget you also have access to the activity solutions if you want to cut and paste some of the rules from our "navigation.css" solution.

2. At the top of your "navigation.css" file, add the following three rules.

```css
/* styles for the overall nav area */
nav {
    background: #717B32 url(nav-gradient.png) repeat-x 0px -15px;
}

/* styles for the top-most list */
nav>ul {
    display: inline-block;
    text-align: center;
    margin: 0;
    padding-top: 8px;
    line-height: 100%;
    width: 800px;
}
```

```
/* styles for all list items anywhere in the nav area */
nav li {
    width: 150px;
    margin: 0;
    padding: 0 0 8px 0;
    float: left;
    position: relative;
    list-style: none;
    z-index: 10;
}
```

The first rule will set up a background gradient image for the entire navigation bar. The second rule will select the one and only direct <**ul**> child of <**nav**> and set several styles. The most important are the **inline-block display** and the width and the text centering. The third rule will select all list items <**li**> within the <**nav**> and set a standard width, margin, and padding. The list items are also floated to the left with relative positioning, given a high **z-index** to stay on top, and the default bullet is removed.

3. Save your changes to "navigation.css" and load "index.html" in Komodo Edit. You need to make one last change before viewing the results in a web browser. The "index.html" page needs to have a link to the new CSS file, so add the following line underneath the existing "global.css" link:

```
<link rel="stylesheet" href="SiteStyle/global.css">
<link rel="stylesheet" href="SiteStyle/navigation.css">

</head>
```

4. Save your changes to "index.html" and reload the page in your web browser to see the results.

The entire <**nav**> bar should have a background gradient image, and we have positioned the list items in a bar from left to right across the top. The secondary lists under each top topic are still visible.

5. Now add another two rules to control the style of the hyperlinks.

```
/* styles for all hyperlinks within the nav area */
nav a {
    padding: 5px 0px;
    margin: 0;
    font-weight: bold;
    font-size: 14px;
    font-variant: normal;
    color: black;
    display: block;
    text-decoration: none;
    text-shadow: 0 1px 0 rgba(255,255,255,1);
}

/* styles for top-level hyperlinks in the top list */
nav>ul>li>a {
    text-shadow: 2px 2px 3px rgba(0,0,0,0.6);
    color: #e7e5e5;
}
```

The first rule will change the hyperlink appearance to remove the underline, add a text shadow, and set some other size and text styles. The second rule will select only the top-level hyperlinks that are a direct child of a list item that is a direct child of **<nav>**. We want to make these top-level hyperlinks a different color with a different text shadow.

6. Save your changes to "navigation.css" and reload "index.html" to see the results.

The top-level links should be a light color with a dark shadow, and the secondary links should be a dark color with a light shadow. For now the list items still spill over into the MainContent area. In the next lesson you'll learn to use ":hover" styles to make the drop-down effect and add more styling to the secondary list items.

Lesson Three: Styling Second-Level Dynamic Menus

In this lesson we're going to finish our dynamic menus by adding special effects to the secondary list items underneath the top row.

Adding Background, Borders, and Shadowing

Our menu will come to life when the user hovers the mouse cursor over one of the top items. The following three rules will change the background color and add some rounded borders and shadowing to highlight the currently selected list item.

```css
/* styles for hovering over any list item within the menu */
nav li:hover {
    background-color: #EDEFEE;
}
/* styles for the top-level list entries in top list, no hover */
nav>ul>li {
    padding: 5px 0px;
    margin: 0;
    font-weight: bold;
    font-size: 20px;
    color: black;
    border-radius: 10px 10px 0 0;
}
/* styles for the top-level list entries in top list, with hover */
nav>ul>li:hover {
    box-shadow: 8px 8px 7px rgba(0,0,0,0.6);
}
```

The first rule selects all list items (both top-level and secondary) in the <**nav**> and sets a new, lighter background color while the mouse is hovering. The second rule styles the first-level list items only (the ones containing the "Home", "Hunter", and "Shadow" anchors). Those items will have a rounded top corners and some larger, bold font. The third rule adds a shadow to the right side of the first-level list items when hovering over them. You can see all three effects in this picture.

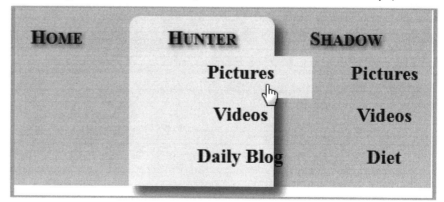

Making "Drop-Down" Effects

In order to get a "drop-down" effect, we need to hide the secondary list <ul> elements by default. Then we need to display them only when the mouse is hovering over the parent list item for the <ul>. These two rules will do exactly that!

```css
/* styles for any second-level list under a top item */
nav li ul {
    display: none;
    margin: 0;
    padding: 0;
    width: 150px;
    position: absolute;
    background: #EDEFEE;
    background-size: 100%;
    border-radius: 0 0 10px 10px;
    box-shadow: 8px 8px 7px rgba(0,0,0,0.6);
    text-shadow: none;
}

/* show the second-level list whenever user hovers over the top list item */
nav li:hover > ul {
    display: block;
}
```

The first rule selects all <ul> elements that are part of some parent <li>; these will be our secondary lists. The **display** is set to *none* which means they will be hidden. The remaining properties will control how the list would appear when it's unhidden with specific margins, padding, backgrounds, and other effects. The second rule simply changes the <ul> display to block when the user hovers the mouse over the parent list item.

Now we're really getting somewhere! As you can see, only the <ul> that the mouse is hovering over is displayed. The others are hidden.

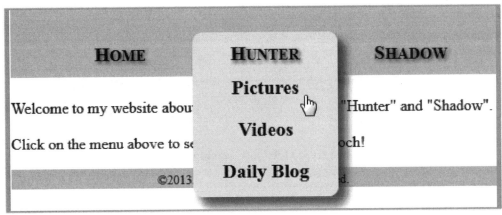

Styling the Secondary List Items

Our secondary list items are a bit boring right now, so let's add some extra styling to show a background image and change the color of a link when hovering.

```css
/* show a background image on each secondary list item */
nav li ul li {
    background: #EDEFEE 0px -3px url(bone.png) no-repeat;
    background-size: 100% 100%;
}
/* if the user is hovering over a second-level link, change its style */
nav li:hover li a:hover {
    color: blue;
}
/* make sure the bottom of the second-level lists stays rounded */
nav>ul>li>ul>li:last-child {
    border-radius: 0 0 10px 10px;
}
```

The first rule selects all list items <li> that are children of a <ul> that itself is a child of a <li>. In other words, we are selecting the individual secondary list items in the drop-down menu and setting a background image. The second rule selects the anchor links <a> when hovering over them, if those links are part of a list item <li> that itself is a child of a parent (top-level) list item. That's a mouthful just to set a new color!

The last rule is a bit complicated. We want to select the last child list item <li> in each secondary list and apply a border-radius style to make sure the bottom corners are rounded to match the top. So you can see we are navigating from the top <nav> down through each <ul> and <li> in the node tree and applying the ":last-child" pseudo-selector to the final <li>.

As you can imagine, even with a node tree drawn out on paper it can take some trial and error to get your CSS selector rules exactly right. You can usually solve the same problem in many

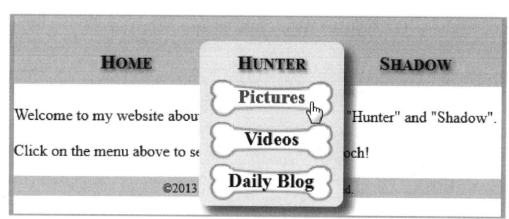

different ways. So if you look online for other examples of drop-down menus, you may find some similarities and some differences in the selectors.

Handling the "#home" Link

There is one last thing to do before we are done. The "Home" link is special because it does not have a

secondary drop-down menu. So some of our earlier styles, including those that round off the bottom corners and change the link color on hover do not apply. If you hover your mouse over our example "Home" link now, you'll see the image to the right.

We want rounded top and bottom corners and we also want to change the text color when the user hovers over the link. It can get very tricky to select just this element and no other with relationships and pseudo-selectors. Fortunately, we were thinking ahead and have already added a unique **id** to the element:

```
<li id="home"><a href="index.html">Home</a>
```

Now we can write a couple of simple CSS rules that target the "home" list item and child hyperlink directly.

```
/* if the user is hovering over the home list item, change its style */
#home:hover {
    border-radius: 10px 10px 10px 10px;
}

/* if the user is hovering over the home link, change its style */
#home a:hover {
    color: blue;
}
```

This is pretty straightforward, and as a result, our "Home" menu item now behaves like a secondary menu with rounded corners and styled hyperlinks that change color on hover.

Our walk-through of the example "My 2 Dogs" dynamic menu shows one way these drop-down effects can be created. There are many possible solutions using a variety of CSS relationships and pseudo-selectors. You may notice that your Aquamaniacs navigation menu does not have exactly the same rules as the example! That's fine, because we want to get some different effects on that website.

Work with Me: Finishing the Aquamaniacs Drop-Down Menus

Let's finish your Aquamaniacs drop-down menus!

1. Run Komodo Edit and open your "navigation.css" file.

2. Scroll down to the bottom and add the following three rules:

```
/* styles for hovering over any list item within the menu */
nav li:hover {
    background-color: #EDEFEE;
}

/* styles for the top-level list entries in top list, no hover */
nav>ul>li {
    border-radius: 10px 10px 0 0;
}

/* styles for the top-level list entries in top list, with hover */
nav>ul>li:hover {
    box-shadow: 8px 8px 7px rgba(0,0,0,0.6);
}
```

The first rule will select all **<nav>** list items when hovering over them and set a common background color. The second rule will select only the top-level list items that are direct children of the top **<ul>** and set rounded corners on the top. The third rule will select those same list items when hovering over them and set up a box-shadow effect.

3. Save your changes to "navigation.css" and reload "index.html". You should see that selected list items now have a different background with rounded corners on top and a shadow to the right.

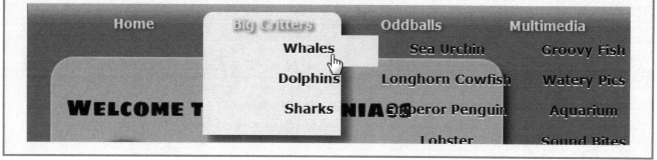

4. Get ready; the next three rules will make a big difference!

```css
/* styles for any second-level list under a top item */
nav li ul {
    display: none;
    margin: 0;
    padding: 0;
    width: 150px;
    position: absolute;
    background: #EDEFEE url(nav-drop.png) no-repeat bottom;
    background-size: 100%;
    border-radius: 0 0 10px 10px;
    box-shadow: 8px 8px 7px rgba(0,0,0,0.6);
    text-shadow: none;
}

/* styles for any second-level list item under a top item */
nav li ul li {
    margin: 0;
    padding: 2px 0;
}

/* show the second-level list whenever user hovers over the top list item */
nav li:hover > ul {
    display: block;
}
```

The first rule selects all secondary lists <ul> and sets the **display** to *none* so they are hidden by default. We also set up several special effects such as a background image, rounded corners and box shadows. The second rule makes some small changes to the margin and padding of the individual list items <li> within the secondary list <ul>. The third rule will change the secondary <ul> **display** to *block* when the user hovers the mouse over the parent list item. This is where the magic happens!

5. Save your changes to "navigation.css" and reload "index.html".

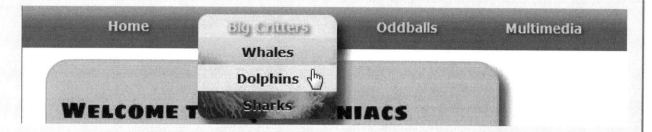

You should see all secondary lists hidden by default until you hover a mouse over one of them. When hovering, the secondary lists have a nice background image. The selected hyperlink doesn't look quite right yet – it has a white background and no other coloring. Also, if you hover over the very last item in a list, we lose the rounded corners on the bottom. We'll fix these things next.

6. At the bottom of "navigation.css", add the following four small rules:

```
/* if the user is hovering over any list item, change its style */
nav li:hover {
    color: black;
}


/* if the user is hovering over a second-level list item, change its style */
nav ul li ul li:hover {
    background-color:rgba(0,0,0,0.0);
}


/* if the user is hovering over a second-level link, change its style */
nav li:hover li a:hover {
    color: #717B32;
}


/* make sure the bottom of the second-level lists stays rounded */
nav>ul>li>ul>li:last-child {
    border-radius: 0 0 10px 10px;
}
```

These rules will change the color of the links when we hover over them, and also set up a completely transparent background image when hovering over a secondary list item. That will allow the background image to shine through. The last rule will select the last <li> child of the secondary list and ensure the bottom corners are rounded.

7. Save your changes to "navigation.css" and reload "index.html". Have we fixed all the problems?

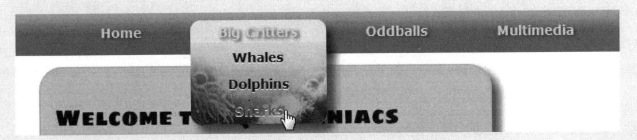

This looks pretty good; our hyperlinks have now changed to a light green color without blocking the background image, and the corners are nicely rounded on the bottom.

8. We need to fix one last thing. Our "home" link shows the same problems described in the lesson text because it does not have a  secondary list. The bottom corners are not rounded and the link text does not change color. Add the following two rules to complete your menu.

```css
/* if the user is hovering over the home list item, change its style */
#home:hover {
    border-radius: 10px 10px 10px 10px;
}


/* if the user is hovering over the home link, change its style */
#home a:hover {
    color: #717B32;
}
```

Our navigation bar already has the **id** property set to "*home*" for the "Home" list item. So the first rule will set rounded top and bottom corners when hovering over that list item. The second rule will change the hyperlink color when hovering directly over the link text.

9. Save your "navigation.css" changes one last time and check out the results.

Congratulations, your Aquamaniacs menus are done and they look great!

Each of your website pages already contains a **<link>** to "navigation.css", so you should be able to navigate through all of the pages that you have created to see the same dynamic menus on each page. Keep in mind that some pages have not yet been created, so selecting those links will give you an error.

Chapter Review

- A **drop-down** or **dynamic** menu allows a website to handle a large navigation section without using huge amounts of space on the page.

- Drop-down menus start with a single small list of items across the top or side. When you hover your mouse over a topic, more options pop-out.

- Dynamic menus can be formed using a combination of lists <li> and CSS styles that use relationship and pseudo-state selectors.

- You can use the `display` property to change the behavior of an element between inline and block, or even hide the element completely.

- A `display` of "none" means the element is hidden completely and does not take up any space.

- A `display` of "inline" means the element will be displayed without any extra spacing or line breaks.

- A `display` value of "block" means the element will be displayed on its own line with extra spacing.

- A `display` value of "inline-block" means the element will be displayed "inline" as a whole, but contents inside the element are treated as a block.

- Drawing a node tree drawn out on paper can help you create your CSS selector rules correctly.

- Adding a unique **id** to the element will allow you to style just that element.

Your Turn Activity: Lionfish

In this activity you are going to create a new "Lionfish" page with a dynamic sidebar. The sidebar will display information instead of providing navigation links, but you can still use our new dynamic concepts to create special effects activated by a mouse.

Your activity requirements and instructions are found in the "Chapter_10_Activity.pdf" document located in your "KidCoder/AdvancedWebDesign/Activity Docs" folder. You can access this document through your Student Menu or by double-clicking on it from Windows Explorer or Mac OS Finder.

Complete this activity now and ensure you understand the material before continuing!

Chapter Eleven: Introducing JavaScript

Users enjoy a dynamic, interactive web page. We've been able to create some special effects with CSS pseudo-states like ":hover", but to really interact with a user you need to learn a new language called **JavaScript**. You will learn to write some simple JavaScript in this chapter.

Lesson One: JavaScript Concepts

So far you have learned about two of the three main areas of web design. Web page **content** includes the HTML elements in your HTML file plus the actual data such as text and images that your user wants to see. The web page **presentation** (appearance and style) is controlled by your CSS rules which are usually stored in a CSS file.

The third main area of web design is **behavior**. Behavior describes how your web pages will interact with the user. That's where **JavaScript** comes in! JavaScript is the name of a programming language that runs in your web browser. As a programming language, JavaScript is quite different than HTML or CSS. With HTML and CSS, you (the website designer) control exactly what the user will see when the page loads. But with JavaScript, you can add **logic** or **behavior** to a page that will run when the page loads or in response to some user event like a mouse or button click.

What can JavaScript Do?

JavaScript is a large topic that could fill an entire book, so we are only going to cover some very simple parts of the language. But professional website designers can use JavaScript for many tasks, including:

- Changing parts of the content or presentation when things happen, such as a mouse click
- Checking to see if the user has entered valid data into forms on the page
- Find information about the local computer and web browser and adjust the page if needed
- Manage web browser "cookies" (small pieces of information left behind by pages on your computer)
- Perform calculations without going back to a web server
- Display pop-up messages
- Open new browser windows and change the status bar contents
- Work with dates, times, and calendars
- …and much, much more!

195

The <script> Element

All JavaScript on your web page must go inside a <script> element.

```
<script>

</script>
```

Unlike other HTML elements, the <script> element can actually be placed both inside the <head> and inside the <body> areas! Sometimes it makes sense to put it in one place or the other, but often a <script> just contains some logic that needs to run at a later time, so it doesn't matter where it goes. For simplicity, you'll usually put all of your scripts together in the same place so they are easy to find and manage.

The "document.write()" Function

Let's get started right away with some JavaScript that will add new content to your HTML page. If you place a <script> in the <body>, that script will be run as the page is being built by the browser. You can use a function called "document.write()" to insert new HTML elements and contents into the page.

```
<body>
    <h1>Welcome to Pizza Palace!</h1>
    <script>
        // output today's date
        document.write("<p><em>Today is Tuesday</em></p>");
    </script>
    <p>What kind of pizza would you like to order?</p>
</body>
```

Welcome to Pizza Palace!

Today is Tuesday

What kind of pizza would you like to order?

The JavaScript inside the <script> element will run when the web browser finds it as the body is being built. The **document.write()** function will add whatever you place inside the quotes directly into your HTML page.

The **syntax** of a language includes the rules you need to carefully follow in order for your code to be valid and to work correctly. The example above shows several important parts of JavaScript syntax.

JavaScript Statements

Most programming languages, including JavaScript, are built around a series of **statements**. A statement is simply one command or piece of logic that is meaningful to the language. When we called the **document.write()** function, that was a single statement.

The example below has two statements.

```
document.write("<p><em>Today is Tuesday</em></p>");
document.write("<p><em>At least it's not Monday!</em></p>");
```

In JavaScript, you should place a semicolon ";" at the end of each statement. That is a signal to the web browser that you have completed one specific command and are about to move to the next one.

JavaScript Comments

You have used comments in both HTML and CSS. They work the same way in JavaScript. A comment is not part of the JavaScript logic and will be ignored by the web browser. You can leave comments to yourself or others in your scripts to explain the purpose of the code or give other information to anyone that reads the code.

```
/* this is where we want to display
   the current date and time to the user */
document.write("<p><em>Today is Tuesday</em></p>");  // output today's date
```

If you want to add a comment to a single line, you can prefix it with two forward slash marks "//". Anything after a "//" to the end of the line becomes a comment. You can also write a longer comment across more than one line. In that case you use a slash and asterisk "/*" at the start of the comment and a closing asterisk and slash "*/" at the end of the comment.

Working with Text

When you want to create text within your JavaScript code, you will surround the text with matching sets of single or double quotes. Either way will work, just make sure you match them up and don't mix styles.

```
<script>
    document.write("Double quotes work just fine");
    document.write('Single quotes also work great');
</script>
```

In programming terms a piece of text in quotes is called a **string**. You can actually build larger strings by adding together smaller strings with the plus sign (+). This example combines three different strings:

```
document.write("<p><em>Today is " + Date() + "</em></p>");
```

The **Date**() function is a quick way to get the current date and time, and adding it together with other strings like this will produce some pretty detailed output.

Welcome to Pizza Palace!

Today is Tue Jan 21 2014 00:31:01 GMT-0500 (Eastern Standard Time)

What kind of pizza would you like to order?

You can see our web page now contains some dynamic content that will change every time a user loads the page! This is much more useful than simply writing out some static text with **document.write**(). Static text can be placed in your HTML directly without using JavaScript, but JavaScript is good for adding dynamic content when needed.

You'll notice the date and time string is pretty complicated, and unfortunately it takes some more effort to make the output easier to read. So we'll just leave this as a quick demonstration of how JavaScript can be used to add new content to a web page.

Keep in mind that JavaScript statements placed in the HTML page will run immediately as the page loads, unless they are wrapped in a function. You'll learn how to write functions in the next lesson. But any **<script>** elements that contain JavaScript statements outside of a function will cause those statements to run as the page is loaded from top to bottom.

Work with Me: Your First JavaScript Commands

You are going to practice your JavaScript skills on a new "Seahorse" Aquamaniacs page. Let's get that page set up now and then write some JavaScript code!

1. Using Windows Explorer or Mac OS Finder, copy the "seahorse.html" file from "Activity Starters/Chapter11/" to your "MyProjects/Aquamaniacs" folder.

2. Also copy the "Activity Starters/Chapter11/PagePhotos/seahorse.jpg" file to your "MyProjects/Aquamaniacs/PagePhotos" folder

3. Load the "seahorse.html" file in your web browser to see the default content. You should have a captioned photo on the left and some paragraph text on the right.

THE SEAHORSE

This odd creature is covered with bony plates and has a tube-like snout. The seahorse does not have scales like other fish. Instead it is covered in little bony plates under a thin layer of skin. This skin blends into its environment so this tiny creature can camouflage itself quite well. It spends its time bobbing in the sea grasses and coral reefs waiting for its favorite meal of zooplankton, small crustaceans, and larval fishes to float by. When their pray gets close enough the seahorse sucks them in through its long snout. Its long tail wraps around the sea grass so it can stay in one place. Hiding secretly and quietly in its shallow garden.

A Seahorse

4. Now, open "seahorse.html" in Komodo Edit go down to the **<footer>** element at the bottom. Add a new **<script>** element as shown below to output the current date and time to the footer.

```
<footer>
    <script>
    document.write("<small>Today is " + Date() + "</small><br />");
    </script>
    <small>&copy;2013. Homeschool Programming. All Rights Reserved.</small>
</footer>
```

Notice we wrapped the output in a **<small>** element to match the existing footer text. We also added a line break **
** at the end to separate the two lines.

5. Save your changes to "seahorse.html" and load the file in your web browser. Does it show the current date and time correctly?

> Today is Sat Jan 25 2014 15:49:51 GMT-0500 (Eastern Standard Time)
> ©2013. Homeschool Programming. All Rights Reserved.

6. You can practice writing other content and elements to the page with new **<script>** elements if you like. They can be placed anywhere in the **<body>**, including the "MainContent" area.

Lesson Two: JavaScript Events and Functions

You will find that using **document.write**() as the page loads has limited usefulness. In order to make the user's experience interactive, you really want to respond to things that the user is doing such as hovering or clicking the mouse, or selecting a button. You might also want to take some action once the page has completely loaded. Things that trigger JavaScript to run in each case are called "**events**".

The <button> Element

The HTML <**button**> element makes a clickable button on your web page. Here is an example:

```
<p>What kind of pizza would you like to order?</p>
<button type="button">Place Order</button>
```

There are a few different kinds of buttons and you don't want to web browser to guess what you want, so always set the **type** attribute equal to "*button*".

Button elements are cool because you can put images inside just like text.

```
<p>What kind of pizza would you like to order?</p>
<button type="button"><img src="pizza_button.png"/></button>
```

Now, a button by itself doesn't do anything. We need to add some JavaScript to respond to the user's button-click event.

To add JavaScript commands to a button click, you will add the **onclick** attribute to the <**button**> element. The value will contain the JavaScript commands to be run when the button is clicked. You don't need to use a <**script**> element; your JavaScript statements can be placed directly inside the attribute value.

```
<button type="button" onclick="document.write('Ready in 30 minutes!');">Place
Order</button>
```

In this example, we want the button to display "Ready in 30 minutes!" when clicked. Notice that we used different kinds of quotes in order to put quoted text inside an attribute value. The outer quotes for **onclick** are double quotes, and the quotes around just the text part are single quotes. That way the web browser can tell where each part starts and stops. You can do it the other way too – single quotes on the outside and double quotes inside. Just make sure you use the matching quote style on each part.

Now, when you actually click a button with this JavaScript, something unexpected will happen! The image on the left shows your page before the click, and the image on the right shows the page afterwards.

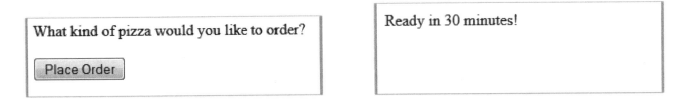

Your entire page has been replaced with just the output from **document.write()**! When this function runs **after** the page has finished loading – perhaps in response to a button click – it will completely replace the entire HTML content of the page. This is probably **not** what you want to happen, so be careful.

Alert Pop-ups

If you just want to display a quick confirmation to the user, you can use the JavaScript **alert()** function. This function will display text in a pop-up box without changing the rest of the page.

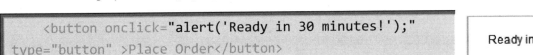

```
<button onclick="alert('Ready in 30 minutes!');"
type="button" >Place Order</button>
```

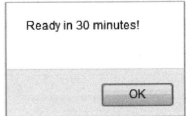

The pop-up message will appear on top of your page and go away when you click the "OK" button. The rest of the page will remain the same.

Events

An **event** is an action the user performs through the browser or the browser does on its own. It works like the word **when** – *when* this happens, *when* they do that, *when* this is finished. We just finished experimenting with the "**onclick**" event that runs *when* a button is clicked. There are several other kinds of events that you may want to use. The table below shows some of the more common events.

JavaScript Event	Description
onclick=	Runs when a user clicks the mouse on the element
onmouseover= onmouseout=	Runs when the user moves the mouse over an element (onmouseover) or moves the mouse away from an element (onmouseout)
onkeydown=	Runs when the user presses a key
onmousedown= onmouseup=	Runs when the user presses the mouse button down (onmousedown) or when the user releases the mouse button (onmouseup)

OK, let's set up cheese and pepperoni pizza images on our ordering page.

```
<p>What kind of pizza would you like to order?</p>
<p><img onclick="alert('Cheese');" src="cheese_pizza.png"/>
   <img onclick="alert('Pepperoni');" src="pepperoni_pizza.png"/></p>
<button type="button" onclick="alert('Ready in 30 minutes!');">Place
Order</button>
```

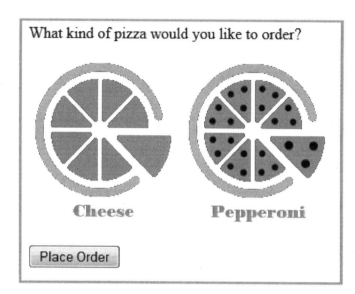

For each <img> element we added an **onclick** attribute with some JavaScript to run if that image is clicked. Clicking on the cheese image will display "Cheese" in a pop-up, and clicking on the pepperoni image will display "Pepperoni".

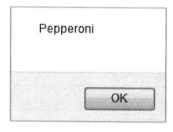

You can easily place these event attributes on most major HTML Elements. You can even add more than one attribute at a time to run a different script on multiple events.

```
<p onmouseover="alert('over');" onmouseup="alert('up');">
   What kind of pizza would you like to order?</p>
```

Here we have added both **onmouseover** and **onmouseup** events to a simple paragraph <p>. Now this doesn't make much sense, and a user would be very confused. But it would work! You would see an "over" alert when the mouse cursor enters the paragraph area. You would also see an "up" message when the user clicks down and then releases the mouse button over the paragraph.

JavaScript Functions

As you can imagine, it would be hard to write many lines of JavaScript code and place them all within an event attribute on an element. Let's say we wanted to run 10 lines of JavaScript when the user clicks on our "Place Order" button. We certainly don't want to write all 10 lines within the **onclick** attribute value; that would be very hard to read, even when each line is separated by semicolons.

```
<button type="button" onclick="Line1;Line2;Line3;...">Place Order</button>
```

To handle this situation you can create a JavaScript **function**. A function is a block of code with one or more JavaScript statements that go together. These statements do not run until the function is called or triggered by some event. Your function contains a list of statements that run in the order that they are written. It's usually clearer if you define your function inside a **<script>** element somewhere on your page, and then **call** or **run** the function from the event attribute.

```
<script>
    function placeOrder()
    {
        // display an alert for the user
        alert('Ready in 30 minutes!');
    }
</script>
<button type="button" onclick="placeOrder();">Place Order</button>
```

To define a function, as shown above, start with the key word "function" inside your **<script>** element. Then add a space and the name of your function. We called our function "placeOrder". Function names should contain only letters and numbers, and no spaces. After the function name comes an opening and closing set of parentheses ( ). It's possible to pass data into this function, but we aren't going to cover any harder programming concepts.

After your function parentheses comes an opening and closing set of curly braces { and }. These curly braces define the **body** of your function. The body contains all of the statements that will run when the function is called. Right now our function body contains only a comment and a single **alert()** statement.

This function will do exactly the same thing as placing the **alert()** command inside the **onclick** attribute. But it's easier to read, and we can easily add more statements and comments inside the curly braces to make a longer function. You can also call one function from many places in your code, so you don't have to write the same set of statements more than once.

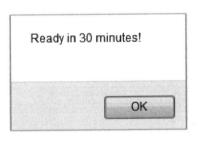

Remember that you can place your **<script>** elements in the **<head>** area as well as the **<body>**. If they don't need to be in a particular place, because they won't run until an event happens, then you can place your **<script>** elements just about anywhere. It's common to group them all together in the **<head>** or at the beginning or end of the **<body>** so they can be found easily.

Writing functions that can be re-used from place to place is a great way to save time and effort. In fact, you can use functions written by other people that do many complicated and wonderful things for you. We'll explore a popular library called **jQuery** in later chapters. jQuery is basically a giant set of JavaScript functions that have already been written to solve many common web design tasks.

 **Work with Me: Waking the Seahorse**

Let's add a button to our "Seahorse" page and display a JavaScript alert when the button is pressed.

1. Run Komodo Edit and load your "seahorse.html" page. Add a new button and JavaScript function at the bottom of the "MainContent" area as shown below.

```
<p>This odd creature is covered with bony plates ...


<script>
    function wakeUp()
    {
        // display an alert for the user
        alert("OK, OK, I'm awake.");
    }
</script>
<div>
  <button type="button" onclick="wakeUp();">Wake Up!</button>
</div>

</div><!-- end of MainContent -->
```

This button will show the text "Wake Up!" and call the "**wakeUp()**" function when clicked. Inside the **wakeUp()** function we simply display an **alert()** to show the seahorse is now awake.

2. Save your "seahorse.html" changes and reload it in your web browser to test the changes.

You should now see a new button near the bottom of the "MainContent" area.

Clicking on the button will show the alert pop-up.

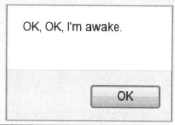

Lesson Three: Managing Elements with JavaScript

JavaScript allows you to control many parts of your web page, including HTML element contents and style. Remember that your web browser builds a node tree from all the elements on your page such as <**body**>, <**h1**>, <**p**>, <**a**>, and so on. This node tree is also called the "Document Object Model" or **DOM**. You might see the term DOM used often by other programmers when describing JavaScript behavior. So if you see DOM, just think "node tree" instead.

Getting HTML Elements by Id

JavaScript contains some handy functions to let you grab elements from your node tree. You can use the **document.getElementById()** function to get an element based on its unique **id** property. Can you figure out what this example will do?

```
<script>
    function selectCheese()
    {
        document.getElementById("cheese").style.border="5px solid red";
    }
</script>
<p><img id="cheese" onclick="selectCheese();" src="cheese_pizza.png"/>
    <img id="pepperoni" src="pepperoni_pizza.png"/></p>
```

We have created a **selectCheese()** JavaScript function that will be called when the user clicks on the first <**img**> element. We gave that element the unique **id** "*cheese*". Now, inside the **selectCheese()** function body we placed a single statement.

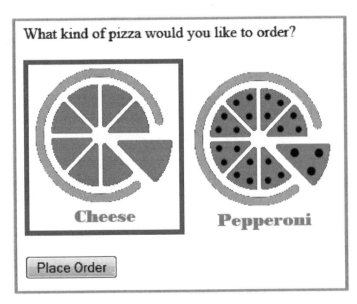

The **document.getElementById**("cheese") statement will search the node tree and find the element with the **id** equal to "cheese" – in this case, that's our first <**img**> element. We then immediately set the border style on that element to have a "*5x solid red*" border.

As you probably guessed, now when the user clicks on the cheese pizza, it will magically gain a solid red border. We now have an interactive web page that gives the user some visual feedback when they do something useful.

The "style" Property

As you just saw, you can use the **style** property on an element in the node tree to control CSS properties for that element. This is a very powerful feature that lets you change your page in creative ways as the user moves through the page.

In order to use the **style** property, you first need to have an element from the node or DOM tree. Once you get that element, add a dot (.) and then the word "**style**". After that, place another dot (.) and then the name of the property you want to change (such as "**border**"). Finally, add an equal sign (=) and then the new value in quotes. Don't forget to end every JavaScript statement with a semicolon!

```
element.style.property="value";
```

You've seen how the *element* in the pattern above can be replaced with **document.getElementById()** to find a specific element by **id**. After that, you just need to find the JavaScript name for the CSS property you want to change. Unfortunately JavaScript property names are not exactly the same as their CSS versions!

The table below shows just a few examples JavaScript property names and the matching CSS properties.

JavaScript property	CSS property
border	border
borderColor	border-color
margin	margin
marginTop	margin-top

Do you see the pattern? JavaScript property names are usually the same for the short, single-word properties. But you can't use a dash (-) in a JavaScript property name, so any CSS property like "border-color" with a dash becomes "borderColor" in JavaScript. The dash is removed and the first letter of the second word is capitalized. This pattern may not hold for all properties, but it's a good starting point.

If you don't want to memorize or guess at JavaScript CSS property names, you can easily find lists of them online by searching for "JavaScript DOM Style Property" or similar keywords. The popular W3Schools website has an excellent reference at http://www.w3schools.com/jsref/dom_obj_style.asp.

Komodo Edit also has some handy built-in helpers that will make suggestions as you type JavaScript commands.

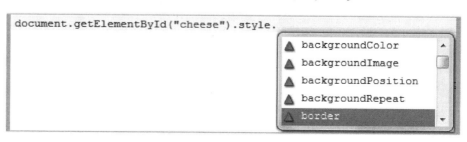

OK, let's create a larger example that will change both the cheese and pepperoni images each time the user clicks on one of them.

```
<script>
    function selectCheese()
    {
        // make the cheese pizza image normal size with a red border
        document.getElementById("cheese").style.border="5px solid red";
        document.getElementById("cheese").style.width="156px";

        // make the pepperoni pizza image smaller with no border
        document.getElementById("pepperoni").style.width="100px";
        document.getElementById("pepperoni").style.border="none";
    }
    function selectPepperoni()
    {
        // make the pepperoni pizza image normal size with a red border
        document.getElementById("pepperoni").style.border="5px solid red";
        document.getElementById("pepperoni").style.width="156px";

        // make the cheese pizza image smaller with no border
        document.getElementById("cheese").style.width="100px";
        document.getElementById("cheese").style.border="none";
    }
</script>
<p><img id="cheese" onclick="selectCheese();" src="cheese_pizza.png"/>
    <img id="pepperoni" onclick="selectPepperoni();"
                                    src="pepperoni_pizza.png"/></p>
```

Now our functions will create a red border around the image that is clicked and restore it to normal size. We will remove any border from the other image and shrink it to a smaller size.

The "innerHTML" Property

You can also use JavaScript to change the text inside of an element. Once you get an element from the node tree with **getElementById()**, you can set the "**innerHTML**" property like this:

```
element.innerHTML="value";
```

Again you'll use **document.getElementById()** to find some unique element in your node tree. Then just set the "**innerHTML**" property equal to any other text that you want to see. This is a complete replacement of everything inside the element, including all nested children! But it will not change the element itself or any attributes of that element.

Let's write a practical example. When the user clicks our "Place Order" button on the pizza ordering page, we don't want them to accidentally click "Place Order" again and end up with two pizzas. So we can use JavaScript to completely replace the "Place Order" button with something else when they click on it.

```
<script>
    function placeOrder()
    {
        // hide the order button so the user can't re-order
        document.getElementById("orderDiv").innerHTML="<p>Order Placed</p>";

        // display an alert for the user
        alert('Ready in 30 minutes!');
    }
</script>
<div id="orderDiv">
    <button type="button" onclick="placeOrder();">Place Order</button>
</div>
```

Notice we added an extra **<div>** with an "**orderDiv**" id around the **<button>** element. When setting **innerHTML** we are replacing the **inside** contents of the selected element. So if we select the parent **<div>** we can completely replace the **<button>**. If we had selected the **<button>** instead, we could only change the "Place Order" text inside the button.

When the user clicks the "Place Order" button, it will be replaced with a paragraph that says "Order Placed". The user cannot place another order because the **<button>** element is gone.

Work with Me: Good Morning Sunshine

Like most animals, the Seahorse gets grouchy if you try to poke him awake too many times. So let's add some code to our **wakeUp()** function to prevent the user from clicking on the button twice. We can also change the photo border to a bright yellow color to show the Seahorse is awake.

1. Run Komodo Edit and load your "seahorse.html" page.
2. Find the **<img>** element within the **<figure>** and add a new **id** attribute as shown below.

```
<figure>
    <img id="seahorseImg" src="PagePhotos/seahorse.jpg" alt="A seahorse."
width="200" height="281">
    <figcaption>A Seahorse</figcaption>
</figure>
```

Now we can find this element when we want to from our JavaScript code.

3. Next, find your **<div>** element surrounding the **<button>** and give it a unique **id** also.

```
<div id="wakeUpButton">
    <button type="button" onclick="wakeUp();">Wake Up!</button>
</div>
```

4. Find your **wakeUp()** function and add two new lines of code. The first will disable the button so it can't be clicked a second time. The second will change the **<img>** border color to yellow.

```
function wakeUp()
{
    // display an alert for the user
    alert("OK, OK, I'm awake.");
    document.getElementById("wakeUpButton").innerHTML=
                          "<p><strong>I am Awake</strong></p>";
    document.getElementById("seahorseImg").style.borderColor="yellow";
}
```

Notice we wrap a second paragraph **<p>** around the new **innerHTML** text, even though the output paragraph **<p>** remains in place. This will avoid the large drop-cap effect normally given to paragraphs that are direct children of the "MainContent" area.

5. Save your "seahorse.html" changes and reload it in your web browser to test the changes. When you click on the button, you should see the same pop-up message. Then after you click "OK" to close the pop-up, the button should be replaced by text, and the image border should change to yellow.

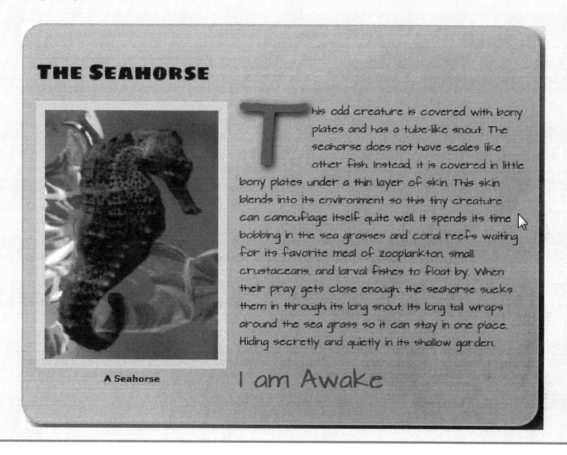

Troubleshooting Steps

It's easy to make a small mistake when writing JavaScript. Often your page will not behave the way you want, or it won't do anything at all! If your JavaScript is not working, try carefully taking these steps:

1. Make sure every opening parenthesis "(" has a matching closing parenthesis ")".
2. Make sure every opening curly brace "{" has a matching closing curly brace "}".
3. Make sure each statement has a semicolon at the end.
4. Make sure your single and double-quotes are correctly matched.
5. If you are not sure if a certain section of script is running at all, try adding an **alert**() pop-up inside.

```
function myfunction()
{
    alert("here I am!");  // verify this code is getting run
}
```

Lesson Four: External JavaScript Files

It is possible to embed CSS rules within an HTML file or place them in an external ".css" file. JavaScript works the same way. You can place your JavaScript functions in a **<script>** element inside an HTML file, or you can put them in a separate ".js" file. We're going to talk about why this is a good idea and show how it is done in this lesson.

The Layers of Web Design

There are three main languages that can be used in web design: HTML, CSS, and JavaScript. Each language adds a layer of richness and complexity to a website. Not surprisingly, each language can also be placed in a separate file.

Layer 1: Content

The **content** layer contains everything required to read and understand the information on a web page. This is the material that the reader wants to find. All of your content goes into your ".html" files.

Layer 2: Presentation

The **presentation** layer controls how the content on a page appears: colors, size, decorations, etc. The presentation is what attracts the reader to the page. Your presentation is defined by CSS rules that go in your ".css" files.

Layer 3: Behavior

The **behavior** layer contains all the instructions on how a web site acts, especially what it does when a reader interacts with it. The behavior is provided by JavaScript, which is a full programming language with many features. JavaScript functions can be placed in your ".js" files.

Why Separate Files?

You can mix your CSS and JavaScript code together into an HTML file, and sometimes that is very convenient. But why might you want to place this code in separate files? There are a number of good reasons, as described in the table on the next page.

Reduce and Re-use	By placing JavaScript in a separate file, you can re-use those functions across many web pages. So you need to type less code into every web page.
Faster Fixes	It is much easier to fix a problem if you can narrow down where to look. With separate files, you know a content problem is in the ".html" file, a presentation problem is in the ".css" style sheet, and a behavioral problem can be found in the ".js" file.
Consistency	On professional web sites, each web page looks and acts the same way – it is **consistent**. Sharing a common style sheet makes it easy to give every page the same appearance. Using a common JavaScript file gives each page the same behavior.
Content Independence	In some cases, readers may turn off your presentation and behavior layers because they just want to get the raw content. By splitting the presentation and behavior into separate files, it becomes very easy to get just the raw content without any presentation or behavior mixed in.
Efficient Downloading	Browsers use a feature called "cache" (pronounced "cash"). A cache is where downloaded files are temporarily stored for future requests. Each time you download a page, all the linked files such as graphics, stylesheets, and JavaScript files are downloaded and stored in the local cache. When you move to the next page in the web site, instead of downloading the same linked files again, the browser checks to see if those files are already in its cache. If they are, the browser uses the local copy of the files instead of downloading another copy. If all your styles and all your behaviors are in shared external files, the browser only has to download those files once. But if you mix your styles and behaviors in with your content, the browser must download that information every time a page is loaded.
Easy Changes	When you use a common external stylesheet, it is really easy to change the look of your web site appearance just by making a change in one place. Everything that links to that shared stylesheet will be affected. The same holds true for behaviors. If your pages link to a shared JavaScript file, then you can change the JavaScript functions in that one file. Your web pages will all then begin behaving according to the new change.

Using External JavaScript Files

To use an external script, your **<script>** tag will contain a link to the external ".js" file instead of the full JavaScript. The **src** attribute contains the JavaScript filename. In the example below we've converted our Pizza Palace ordering screen to use an external JavaScript file named "pizza-palace.js".

```
<script src="pizza-palace.js"></script>
<div id="orderDiv">
    <button type="button" onclick="placeOrder();">Place Order</button>
</div>
```

Your "pizza-palace.js" file would then contain the full JavaScript code without any surrounding **<script>** elements.

```
function placeOrder()
{
    // hide the order button so the user can't re-order
    document.getElementById("orderDiv").innerHTML="<p>Order Placed</p>";

    // display an alert for the user
    alert('Ready in 30 minutes!');
}
```

Your web page will still behave exactly the same way, because it is running the same JavaScript function. But now that function lives in a separate external file that you can manage outside of the HTML file.

Keeping it Neat with a JavaScript Directory

You might create a "**SiteStyle**" sub-folder from your root directory to hold all your CSS stylesheets. This keeps them separated from the HTML files and easier to find. For the same reason you can create a "**Scripts**" directory to hold your JavaScript files. There is nothing special about either of these names, so you might see other websites with folders named "js" and "css" to hold those types of files.

```
<script src="Scripts/pizza-palace.js"></script>
```

If you do place your JavaScript files in a sub-directory, make sure you change your **src** attribute on the **<script>** element to match the new location relative to the HTML page.

Creating External JavaScript files with Komodo Edit

You can use Komodo Edit to create a new JavaScript file for you. From within Komodo Edit, find the directory in your project folder such as such as "Scripts" where the new file will go. Right-click on that directory and select "New File from Template".

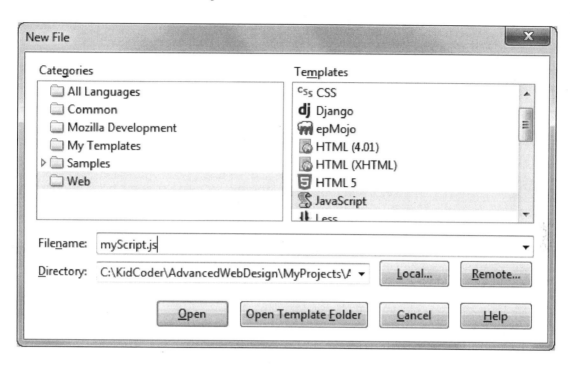

Select "Web" from the Categories on the left, and scroll down to select "JavaScript" from the Templates on the right. Type in your new filename such as "myScript.js", including the ".js" extension, and click "Open" to create your new file.

You should see your new file immediately in the project folder, and you can open it in the center editing area to start adding your JavaScript functions.

Chapter Review

- **JavaScript** is the name of a programming language that runs in your web browser.

- JavaScript can do many things, including changing parts of the page, responding to events, checking for valid data, managing "cookies", and displaying pop-up messages on the screen.

- All JavaScript on your web page must go inside a **<script>** element. This element can be placed inside the **<head>** and **<body>** areas of a web page.

- The "**document.write**()" JavaScript function can be used to insert new HTML elements and contents into a web page.

- A programming **statement** is simply one piece of logic that is meaningful to the language.

- In JavaScript, you should place a semicolon ";" at the end of each statement.

- A JavaScript comment is not part of the JavaScript logic and is ignored by the web browser.

- A single comment line is started with double slash marks (//) and a multi-line comment starts with (/*) and ends with (*/).

- In programming terms a piece of text in quotes is called a **string**.

- The HTML **<button>** element makes a clickable button on your web page.

- The **alert**() function displays text in a pop-up without changing the rest of the page.

- Adding the `onclick` attribute to a **<button>** element will attach JavaScript code to that button.

- You can use many different JavaScript events to add functionality to your web page, like "onclick", "onmouseover", "onmousedown" and "onkeydown".

- A **function** is a block of code with one or more JavaScript statements that go together.

- The **document.getElementById**() function will access an element based on its unique **id** property.

- You can't use a dash (-) in a JavaScript property name, so "border-color" becomes "borderColor".

- Use the **innerHTML** JavaScript property to change the entire inside content of an element.

- Use the **style** JavaScript property to change a CSS property for an element.

- You can place your JavaScript functions in a **<script>** element inside a HTML file, or you can put them in a separate ".js" file.

Your Turn Activity: Cuttlefish

In this activity you are going to create a new "Cuttlefish" page with several JavaScript features.

Your activity requirements and instructions are found in the "Chapter_11_Activity.pdf" document located in your "KidCoder/AdvancedWebDesign/Activity Docs" folder. You can access this document through your Student Menu or by double-clicking on it from Windows Explorer or Mac OS Finder.

Complete this activity now and ensure you understand the material before continuing!

Chapter Twelve: Dynamic Pages with jQuery

You can write complex JavaScript code to do many wonderful things. Fortunately, other programmers have already done some hard work to create interesting JavaScript functions you can use on your website. In this chapter, we are going to explore **jQuery**, a popular JavaScript library.

Lesson One: The jQuery Library

A JavaScript **library** is a set of pre-written JavaScript functions that you can use on your web page. Libraries are stored in external ".js" files that you simply need to link into a web page with a **<script>** element. JavaScript libraries can do things in a well-defined way, hiding all cross-browser differences inside the library. Many JavaScript libraries are free for anyone to use and change.

jQuery

jQuery is a JavaScript library contained within a single file with a name like "jquery-1.11.0.js". The numbers "1.11.0" represent the version and may change over time. jQuery is an open source project and is free to use by anyone. Other JavaScript libraries also exist, but jQuery is popular and used by many large companies like Google, WordPress, Mozilla, Microsoft, Adobe, Apple, Dell, Netflix, and CBS.

The jQuery home page can be found here: http://jquery.com/

jQuery has functions for many common JavaScript tasks, as well as some of the more complicated ones. If you use jQuery, instead of having to write out all that JavaScript yourself, you can simply call the jQuery function with a single line of code. The jQuery library has functions to do many different things, including:

- Changing, adding, or deleting HTML elements
- Searching and selecting elements from the node tree
- Managing CSS styles
- Triggering on events
- Adding special effects and animation
- Managing data, forms, and other new features such as Ajax (allowing your page to fetch data from a server without forcing a full page reload).

You can find a full list of jQuery functions here: http://api.jquery.com/

Using the jQuery Library

Any page that wants to use a jQuery function must first link to the library with a **<script>** element. Since external script files usually just contain a collection of functions that will be called on some event, you don't need to locate this element anywhere inside the **<body>**. You will often see external JavaScript files listed in the **<head>** area instead.

```
    <script src="jquery-1.11.0.js"></script>
</head>
```

Of course, if you have placed the library file in a subdirectory like "Scripts", then use that relative path:

```
    <script src="Scripts/jquery-1.11.0.js"></script>
</head>
```

This is no different than linking to one of your own external JavaScript files. You simply download the file from somewhere else instead of creating it on your own. Your course files will already contain a copy of the jQuery ".js" file so you don't need to fetch your own copy. But if you ever want to get the latest version, you can download it from the jQuery website: http://jquery.com/download/.

Compressed jQuery Library Files

The jQuery library is very large, so comes in two different versions:

- A "development" version, over 250 KB in size
- A "production" version, under 100KB in size

Both versions contain exactly the same JavaScript functions. In the smaller "production" version, all of the comments and whitespace has been removed to make it smaller. So it's still easy for a computer to read, but humans will have a hard time understanding the file. The "development" version keeps all of the extra spacing and comments so human developers can read and understand the functions if needed.

If you see a jQuery filename with "min" somewhere inside, like "jquery.1.11.0.min.js", that is the smaller production version. We will be using the larger development version for our websites. But don't be surprised if you see professional websites linking to a "min" file that is hard to read.

Linking to a Hosted jQuery Library

The jQuery library is so popular that a copy of it is kept on several major online hosts such as Google, Microsoft, or jQuery itself. Instead of downloading and keeping a copy on your own website, you can actually just link directly to one of those versions hosted online.

Just use the full URL of the online version in your **src** attribute like this:

```
<script src="http://code.jquery.com/jquery-1.11.0.min.js"></script>
```

Now when your web users come to your site, their browsers will pull the ".js" file from the other online location instead of your server. Why is this helpful? The biggest reason is that web browser programs will store (cache) copies of files on the local computer. So if it already has a copy of "jquery-1.11.0.min.js" from a particular location, it will not need to go fetch it again! Your web pages will load faster for users that have already visited sites that are using the same jQuery file that you are. Since jQuery is so popular, the odds are good that your users already have a cached copy of this file.

jQuery Versions

Like all software, the jQuery library will have new versions released by the authors from time to time. While the current version is "1.11.0", newer versions may be released by the time you want to use the library yourself. That's OK! In most cases the newer libraries will keep working exactly the same way as the older ones, but they might include some bug fixes or new features.

You can even keep using an older version of the library if you prefer. So long as you have a copy of the older library on your website, or can find a link to it hosted online, you can keep using the old library. But it's usually a good idea to upgrade to the latest version every once in a while to keep up with the newest fixes, features, and browser changes.

Work with Me: Getting Started with Funny Fish 2

Throughout this chapter you are going to be working with the "Funny Fish 2" page on your Aquamaniacs site. That page doesn't exist yet, so let's create it now and make sure it has access to the jQuery library.

1. Using Windows Explorer or Mac OS Finder, copy the following files from your Activity Starter directory into your Aquamaniacs project:
   - Copy "Chapter12/funnyfish2.html" to your "Aquamaniacs" folder
   - Copy "Chapter12/Scripts/jquery-1.11.0.js" to your "Aquamaniacs/Scripts" folder
   - Copy "Chapter12/SiteStyle/funnyfish2.css" to your "Aquamaniacs/SiteStyle" folder.
2. Load "funnyfish2.html" into your web browser to see the default page

None of the buttons work yet; it will be your job over the next few lessons to write the JavaScript code for each button. The HTML page already contains a link to the jQuery library you copied into the "Aquamaniacs/Scripts" folder.

Lesson Two: jQuery Syntax and Page Loading

Do you remember the JavaScript we placed inside our example HTML to manage the "Place Order" button on the Pizza Palace screen?

Place Order

```
<script src=" Scripts/pizza-palace.js"></script>
<div id="orderDiv">
    <button type="button" onclick="placeOrder();">Place Order</button>
</div>
```

This works fine, but notice that we had to mix JavaScript in with HTML. Our HTML <**button**> element needs to have an event attribute (**onclick**) set up with a small JavaScript statement ("***placeOrder();***") to kick things off. This makes it harder to read, and ideally we'd like to keep our **content** and our **behavior** as separated as possible. Fortunately, jQuery allows us to attach JavaScript events and commands to HTML elements after the page loads.

The Document Ready Method

When the web browser is loading your HTML page, it takes a bit of time to build the node tree. If your node tree is not fully formed, a JavaScript command may not be able to find elements by id or other selector. So you usually want to let the page load completely before trying to run any JavaScript commands.

You can add JavaScript statements using jQuery that will run once the node tree has been fully loaded. In your script, you would add the following lines:

```
$(document).ready(function() {
  // statements in here will run once the page has fully loaded
});
```

This looks a bit odd, so let's break it down piece-by-piece.

```
$(document).ready(function() {
  // statements in here will run once the page has fully loaded
});
```

The first part, "$", is how you begin making a jQuery function call. The "$" is short for "jQuery". The next part in parentheses, "(document)", tells the jQuery function what to select. So "$(document)" means run a jQuery function on the whole document.

```
$(document).ready(function() {
  // statements in here will run once the page has fully loaded
});
```

The next part, ".ready( )", contains a dot, a function name like "ready", plus opening and closing parentheses and a semicolon to show the end of the JavaScript statement. There are many functions you can call when jQuery has selected something, and **ready()** will cause the function inside the parentheses to run when the document's node tree has fully loaded.

```
$(document).ready(function() {
  // statements in here will run once the page has fully loaded
});
```

The part inside the **ready()** parentheses is the most unusual. Here we have actually defined a full JavaScript function that has no name, simply by declaring a "function()" followed by opening and closing curly braces to mark the beginning and end of the function. Any other statements in-between the curly braces will be part of that function and will run when the page loads.

Let's revisit our Pizza Place ordering page and split apart the JavaScript behavior into a separate file. First we would add this "$(document).ready()" function to our "pizza-place.js" file:

```
$(document).ready(function() {
document.getElementById("orderButton").setAttribute("onclick","placeOrder();");
});
```

Then all that remains in the HTML file is:

```
<script src=" Scripts/pizza-palace.js"></script>
<div id="orderDiv">
    <button id="orderButton" type="button">Place Order</button>
</div>
```

We took the **onclick** attribute and JavaScript value entirely out of the HTML file and placed it in our JavaScript file instead. When the page loads the jQuery "$(document).ready()" function runs and sets the button's **onclick** attribute equal to the "*placeOrder();*" statement.

We are adding behavior to a page after the page loads! The behavior the user can see is still exactly the same. When the button is clicked the **placeOrder()** JavaScript function will run. But we have cleanly separated the content and behavior into separate files.

Ready in 30 minutes!

OK

The jQuery Selector, Setting HTML attributes, and Setting CSS Properties

In the last example we started our jQuery statement with "$(document)". The value in parentheses can actually be any CSS selector that you already know, including element name, class, id, pseudo-selectors, and so on. jQuery has built-in support for applying CSS selectors to the node tree to find elements.

Here are some example selectors:

```
$("p")        // Select all <p> elements on your web page
$("#fish")    // Select all id="fish" elements on your web page
$(".whales")  // Select all class="whales" elements on your web page
```

Therefore, we can simplify our Pizza Palace "$(document).ready()" function by using a jQuery function instead of a normal JavaScript **getElementById()** function.

```
document.getElementById("orderButton").setAttribute("onclick","placeOrder();");
$("#orderButton").attr("onclick","placeOrder();");
```

The second line does exactly the same thing as the first: find the "orderButton" by id, and then set the **onclick** attribute equal to "*placeOrder();*". But it's shorter and a bit faster to read, once you get used to jQuery syntax. Notice we are calling the **attr()** function instead of **ready()**. The **attr()** jQuery function will set an attribute on the selected elements using the provided name and value.

Keep in mind that using CSS selectors may result in more than one element getting found. The jQuery function will apply to all selected elements. So this example will find all paragraphs **<p>** and set the CSS property **color** equal to "*red*":

```
$("p").css("color","red");
```

The job of the **css()** jQuery function, as you might have guessed, is to set the CSS property on all selected elements to the given name and value.

Welcome to Pizza Palace!

Today is Tue Jan 28 2014 01:11:50 GMT-0500 (Eastern Standard Time)

What kind of pizza would you like to order?

Matching Quotation Marks

Both JavaScript and jQuery use the same single or double quotes to surround values. You can either use a set of single quotes around values or a set of double quotes. You cannot start with one style and end with another! Most designers have a favorite and just use one type.

You may get into situations where you need quotes inside of a value. Then you can use one style of quotes around the overall value and the other kind of quotes inside.

Consider these examples.

```
$("#orderButton").attr("onclick","alert( 'Say cheese!' );");    // OK
$("#orderButton").attr("onclick",'alert( "Say cheese!" );');    // OK
$("#orderButton").attr("onclick","alert( "Say cheese!" );");    // ERROR
$("#orderButton").attr("onclick","alert( 'Say cheese!" );');    // ERROR
```

The first statement works fine, because we have a matched set of double quotes on the outside of the value and single quotes when needed inside the value. Likewise the second statement uses a matched set of single quotes on the outside and double quotes on the inside, which is also OK.

However the last two statements will not produce good results. The third line uses all double quotes, so it's hard to tell where the overall value stops and starts. The fourth line has a mixture of quotes, but they are not matched up with the same style on the outside or the inside.

Always use straight quotes like " or ' and never use the fancy curly quotes " or ', which won't work.

Work with Me: Funny Fish 2 Page Loading

Let's add some JavaScript and jQuery behavior to our Funny Fish 2 page. Since we don't want the behavior for this page anywhere else, our first step is to create a new JavaScript file just for this page.

1. In Komodo Edit, select the "Scripts" folder, right-click, and select "New File from Template". Pick the "Web" category and the "JavaScript" template and give it the name "funnyfish2.js". Then click "Open" to create the file.

2. Now, in your new "funnyfish2.js" file, add a function that will be run when the document loads.

```
$(document).ready(function () {
   alert("Welcome to the Funny Fish Frenzy");

});
```

3. Save your "funnyfish2.js" file and load "funnyfish2.html" in your web browser. Did anything happen? No, we forgot a step!

4. We need to link our new script file from the HTML page. So open your "funnyfish2.html" file in Komodo Edit and look in the **<head>** area to find the existing **<script>** element linking to the jQuery library. Underneath that, add a new **<script>** to link to our "funnyfish2.js" file.

```
<script src="Scripts/jquery-1.11.0.js"></script>
<script src="Scripts/funnyfish2.js"></script>

</head>
```

5. Now save your "funnyfish2.html" changes and reload it in a web browser. You should see an alert pop-up as soon as the page loads.

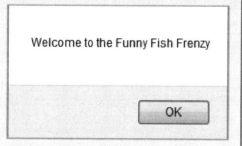

6. Next, return to your "funnyfish2.js" file. Let's add some more behavior to the "$(document).ready()" function to select your paragraph <p> elements and change the styles.

Add the two new lines below to select paragraphs on the page and set the **font-weight** and **font-variant** properties to new values.

```
$(document).ready(function () {
    alert("Welcome to the Funny Fish Frenzy");


    $("p").css("font-weight","bold");
    $("p").css("font-variant","small-caps");

});
```

7. Save your "funnyfish2.js" changes and reload "funnyfish2.html" in your browser. You should see the paragraph text on the right change to bold, small-caps styling.

228

Lesson Three: jQuery Events

jQuery allows you to easily write code to respond to events like button clicks. Each of the normal event attributes such as "**onclick**" has a matching jQuery function you can call to set that event. Instead of manually setting the attribute value like this:

```
$("#orderButton").attr("onclick","placeOrder();");
```

You could call the jQuery **click**() function, passing in your own function definition like this:

```
$("#orderButton").click(function() {placeOrder();} );
```

These two statements seem to be about the same size with a single, simple statement as the action. But in the second case you can easily define a more complicated function:

```
$("#orderButton").click(function() {
        // hide the order button so the user can't re-order
        $("#orderDiv").html("<p>Order Placed</p>");

        // display an alert for the user
        alert('Ready in 30 minutes!');
    }
);
```

Here we have put the entire body of the **placeOrder**() function right into the jQuery **click**() event, so we don't need to define a **placeOrder**() function anywhere else at all!

Notice we introduced another useful jQuery function at the same time: **html**(). This works like the JavaScript **innerHTML** property, replacing the entire contents inside the element with a new string. So the first line will use jQuery to select the "#orderDiv" element and then call the **html**() function to replace the inner content with the new paragraph.

Each of the JavaScript events you have already learned about has a matching jQuery function. Calling that event function will attach a new function to the event, and that function will be run when the event is triggered. The table below shows the common JavaScript events and matching jQuery function names.

jQuery Function	JavaScript Event	Description
click()	onclick=	Runs when a user clicks the mouse on the element
mouseover() mouseout()	onmouseover= onmouseout=	Runs when the user moves the mouse over an element (onmouseover) or moves the mouse away from an element (onmouseout)
keydown()	onkeydown=	Runs when the user presses a key
mousedown() mouseup()	onmousedown= onmouseup=	Runs when the user presses the mouse button down (onmousedown) or when the user releases the mouse button (onmouseup)

Let's re-work our pizza ordering example to use only jQuery functions that are attached to the HTML elements after the document loads. Our HTML file would contain just HTML elements:

```html
<p>What kind of pizza would you like to order?</p>

<p><img id="cheese" src="cheese_pizza.png"/>
    <img id="pepperoni" src="pepperoni_pizza.png"/></p>

<div id="orderDiv">
    <button id="orderButton" type="button">Place Order</button>
</div>
```

Somewhere in the HTML file, possibly in the <**head**>, we need to link to our external JavaScript file:

```html
<script src="Scripts/pizza-place.js"></script>
```

Now, in our "pizza-place.js" file, we need to attach JavaScript commands to our button and images to get the same behavior.

 When writing JavaScript functions, always make sure every opening parenthesis (is matched with a closing parenthesis). Also make sure every opening curly brace { is matched with a closing curly brace }. It's easy to get lost over many lines of code, and forgetting to match opening and closing symbols is a common error.

Our "pizza-place.js" file will contain the following script:

```javascript
// this function will run when the page has loaded
$(document).ready(function() {

    // attach a JavaScript function to the click event on the orderButton
    $("#orderButton").click(function()
     {
         // hide the order button so the user can't re-order
         $("#orderDiv").html("<p>Order Placed</p>");

         // display an alert for the user
         alert('Ready in 30 minutes!');
     });

    // attach a JavaScript function to the click event on the cheese img
    $("#cheese").click(function()
     {
         // make the cheese pizza image normal size with a red border
         $("#cheese").css("border","5px solid red");
         $("#cheese").css("width","156px");

         // make the pepperoni pizza image smaller with no border
         $("#pepperoni").css("width","100px");
         $("#pepperoni").css("border","none");
     });

    // attach a JavaScript function to the click event on the pepperoni img
    $("#pepperoni").click(function()
     {
         // make the pepperoni pizza image normal size with a red border
         $("#pepperoni").css("border","5px solid red");
         $("#pepperoni").css("width","156px");

         // make the cheese pizza image smaller with no border
         $("#cheese").css("width","100px");
         $("#cheese").css("border","none");
     });

}); // end of document ready function
```

This code will do the same thing as our examples in the last chapter, except we have split all of the **behavior** logic out into a separate file, and the HTML file contains just HTML **content**.

Troubleshooting Steps – New and Improved

If your JavaScript or jQuery code is not working correctly, you have probably made a small mistake or typo somewhere in your code. Try carefully taking these steps to find the error:

1. Make sure every opening parenthesis "(" has a matching closing parenthesis ")".
2. Make sure every opening curly brace "{" has a matching closing curly brace "}".

Parentheses and curly braces are used to mark the beginning and ending of functions and parameters, so if they are not matched correctly the web browser will be unable to run your JavaScript successfully!

3. Make sure your single and double-quotes are correctly matched.
4. Make sure your CSS selector in the **$( )** area is correct. If you are selecting by **id**, make sure you add a "#" in front of the name. For example, **$("cheese")** will not select anything, while **$("#cheese")** will select the element with the "*cheese*" **id**.
5. If you want things to happen when the page loads, then you need to wrap your script commands in the jQuery **$(document).ready()** statement. Make sure your **function()** parameter to the **ready()** has opening and closing curly braces and matches our examples exactly.
6. Make sure each statement has a semicolon at the end.
7. If you are not sure if a certain section of script is running at all, try adding an **alert()** pop-up inside.

```
$("#cheese").click(function()
{
    alert("here I am!");  // verify click function is getting called
});
```

Work with Me: Funny Fish 2 Page Events

Now that you know how to attach JavaScript to buttons using jQuery, let's prepare our Funny Fish 2 page to receive button click events.

In your "funnyfish2.html" page, the code creating the "Hide", "Show", and "Toggle" buttons is shown below. These buttons each have a unique **id** we can use to select them from our scripts.

```html
<div class="funnyfish2">
    <button id="hide">Hide</button>
    <button id="show">Show</button>
    <div id="funnyfish2_1">Hide | Show</div>
</div>

<div class="funnyfish2">
    <div id="funnyfish2_2">Toggle</div>
    <button id="toggle">Toggle</button>
</div>
```

1. Edit your "funnyfish2.js" script in Komodo Edit. Inside the existing "$(document).ready()" function, add the following statements to create "click" functions for these three buttons.

```javascript
$("p").css("font-weight","bold");
$("p").css("font-variant","small-caps");

$("#hide").click(function () {
   alert("hide");
});

$("#show").click(function () {
   alert("show");
});

$("#toggle").click(function () {
   alert("toggle");
});
});
```

2. Save your "funnyfish2.js" file and reload it in the web browser. Click on the Hide, Show, and Toggle buttons confirm you get the correct alert pop-up in each case.

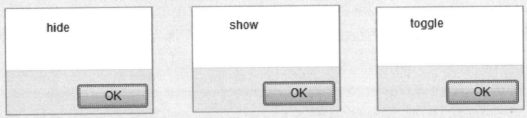

You'll learn how to write the behavior for hide, show, and toggle in the next lesson, so for now these alert pop-ups are just placeholders.

3. Edit your "funnyfish2.js" file again and add two more behaviors. We want the paragraph to have a fancy text shadow when the mouse is hovering over it. When the mouse is over the paragraph (**mouseover**) we add a yellow shadow, and we remove the shadow when the mouse leaves the paragraph (**mouseout**).

```javascript
$("#toggle").click(function () {
    alert("toggle");
});


$("p").mouseover(function () {
    $("p").css("text-shadow","2px 2px yellow");
});


$("p").mouseout(function () {
    $("p").css("text-shadow","none");
});
});
```

4. Save your changes to "funnyfish2.js" and reload "funnyfish2.html" to see the results. The image on the left shows the paragraph with the mouse hovering and a yellow text shadow. The image on the right shows the paragraph once the mouse has left.

CLICK ON A BUTTON TO THE LEFT TO MAKE THE FISH HIDE, APPEAR, OR FADE IN AND OUT.

CLICK ON A BUTTON TO THE LEFT TO MAKE THE FISH HIDE, APPEAR, OR FADE IN AND OUT.

Lesson Four: Hiding and Showing Elements

So far you've used jQuery to do the same sorts of things you could already do with normal JavaScript, but in a cleaner and more organized manner. Of course, many jQuery functions are more powerful than standard CSS properties or JavaScript statements. We'll start learning some of these jQuery functions in this lesson.

Using hide() and show() jQuery Functions

You can use the jQuery **hide**() and **show**() functions to make elements appear and disappear. To demonstrate, let's add a third option to our pizza ordering screen. Everyone likes breadsticks, so we have added a breadstick image and two buttons to add or remove breadsticks from the order.

```html
<p><img id="cheese" src="cheese_pizza.png"/>
    <img id="pepperoni" src="pepperoni_pizza.png"/>
    <img id="breadsticks" src="breadsticks.png"/>
</p>

<div id="orderDiv">
    <button id="orderButton" type="button">Place Order</button>
    <button id="addBreadsticksButton" type="button">Add Breadsticks</button>
    <button id="removeBreadsticksButton" type="button">Remove
                                        Breadsticks</button>
</div>
```

We still have all the same elements and JavaScript as before, but now the HTML contains two new buttons and a breadsticks image.

However, we don't want to show both buttons at the same time, and we don't want to show the breadsticks image until a button is clicked. So let's hide one of the buttons and the image as soon as the page loads.

We can do this inside the "$(document).ready()" function with the following **hide()** commands:

```
// hide the breadsticks button and image by default
$("#removeBreadsticksButton").hide();
$("#breadsticks").hide();
```

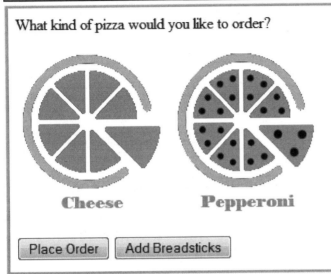

Now when the page loads the breadsticks image is hidden and we see only the "Add Breadsticks" button.

At first this doesn't seem any different than setting the CSS display property to "none", and that's exactly right. By default **hide()** and **show()** will instantly hide or show the element.

However, you can add some parameters inside the parentheses to make **hide()** and **show()** move at different speeds. The parameters "slow" and "fast" will make the element appear or disappear slowly or quickly. The code below adds some **click()** behavior to each button. The "Add" button will make the breadsticks image slowly appear, hide itself, and show the "Remove" button. The "Remove" button will make the breadsticks image quickly disappear, hide itself, and show the "Add" button again.

```
// attach a JavaScript function to the click event on the add button
$("#addBreadsticksButton").click(function()
{
    // make the breadsticks image appear slowly
    $("#breadsticks").show("slow");
    $("#addBreadsticksButton").hide();
    $("#removeBreadsticksButton").show();
});
// attach a JavaScript function to the click event on the remove button
$("#removeBreadsticksButton").click(function()
{
    // make the breadsticks image hide quickly
    $("#breadsticks").hide("fast");
    $("#addBreadsticksButton").show();
    $("#removeBreadsticksButton").hide();
});
```

Now, clicking on the "Add Breadsticks" button will make the image slowly appear and replace the "Add" button with the "Remove" button.

Clicking on "Remove Breadsticks" will make the image hide and change "Remove" back to "Add".

If the "slow" and "fast" options don't give you the exact speed you need, you can enter a number instead such as 1000. This tells the browser how many milliseconds to spend showing or hiding. So 500 means 0.5 seconds, 1000 means 1.0 seconds, and 2000 means 2.0 seconds.

```
$("#breadsticks").hide(2000);    // take 2 seconds to hide the element
```

As we have shown above, you don't need to put quotes around the number.

Using the toggle() jQuery Function

It can be a bit of a pain to write two different JavaScript functions to turn something off and on. Fortunately, jQuery supports a **toggle()** function that will automatically hide an element that is showing or show an element that is hiding. Just like **hide()** and **show()**, you can toggle things instantly with no parameters or use "slow" or "fast" or a number such as 1000 inside the parentheses.

We can use the **toggle()** function to re-write our breadsticks JavaScript with less code.

```
// hide the breadsticks button and image by default
$("#removeBreadsticksButton").hide();
$("#breadsticks").hide();

// attach a JavaScript function to the click event on the add button
$("#addBreadsticksButton,#removeBreadsticksButton").click(function()
  {
     // make the breadsticks image toggle slowly
     $("#breadsticks").toggle("slow");
     $("#addBreadsticksButton").toggle();
     $("#removeBreadsticksButton").toggle();
  });
```

Here we have attached the JavaScript code to both the Add and Remove buttons by using both IDs in the selector. Inside the function we simply **toggle**() the breadsticks image and each button. So whatever was hidden will be displayed and whatever was showing will be hidden. Our pizza screen will work just like before, but we have written less code to get the same behavior.

Work with Me: Funny Fish 2 Hide, Show, and Toggle

You've already done most of the hard work getting the Funny Fish 2 page ready for button click events. The functions are already in your "funnyfish2.js" file with some **alert**() messages as placeholders. Now you are going to replace the alert messages with some jQuery **hide**(), **show**() and **toggle**() commands.

1. Load your "funnyfish2.js" file in Komodo Edit. Find the three functions that run when the buttons are clicked.
2. Edit each function as shown below to replace the **alert**() statements with **hide**(), **show**(), and **toggle**() commands.

```
$("#hide").click(function () {
    alert("hide");
    $("#funnyfish2_1").hide("slow");
});

$("#show").click(function () {
    alert("show");
    $("#funnyfish2_1").show("fast");
});

$("#toggle").click(function () {
    alert("toggle");
    $("#funnyfish2_2").toggle(1500);
});
```

3. Save your "funnyfish2.js" changes and reload "funnyfish2.html" in your web browser. Test out each of your three buttons! Clicking "Hide" will hide the first fish, as shown to the bottom left. Clicking "Show" will restore it again. Then, clicking "Toggle" will hide and show the second fish.

Notice the speed that each fish moves should match the parameters we gave to **hide()**, **show()**, and **toggle()**. You can play with these parameters on your own to experiment with different speeds for each button.

Chapter Review

- A JavaScript **library** is a set of pre-written JavaScript functions that you can use on your web page.
- **jQuery** is a JavaScript library contained within a single file with a name like "jquery-1.11.0.js".
- The jQuery library has functions to do many different things, including modifying HTML elements, triggering on events, and adding special effects and animations.
- jQuery comes in two different files: a large development version and a smaller production version.
- jQuery allows us to attach JavaScript events and commands to HTML elements after the page loads.
- The "$" in a jQuery statement is short for "jQuery".
- The **$(document).ready()** statement will cause the function inside the parentheses to run when the web page's node tree has fully loaded.
- jQuery has built-in support for applying CSS selectors to the node tree to find elements.
- Both JavaScript and jQuery use the same single or double quotes to surround values.
- jQuery allows you to easily write code to respond to events like button clicks.
- The **jQuery html()** function works like the JavaScript **innerHTML** property.
- If your JavaScript or jQuery code is not working correctly, you have probably made a small mistake or typo somewhere in your code.
- You can use the jQuery **hide()** and **show()** functions to make elements appear and disappear.
- You can add parameters inside the parentheses to make **hide()** and **show()** move at different speeds.
- The jQuery **toggle()** function will automatically hide an element that is showing or show an element that is hiding.

Your Turn Activity: Otters

In this activity you are going to create a new "Otters" page to show off some of your new jQuery skills.

Your activity requirements and instructions are found in the "Chapter_12_Activity.pdf" document located in your "KidCoder/AdvancedWebDesign/Activity Docs" folder. You can access this document through your Student Menu or by double-clicking on it from Windows Explorer or Mac OS Finder.

Complete this activity now and ensure you understand the material before continuing!

Chapter Thirteen: jQuery Special Effects

In this chapter we are going to continue exploring some of the special effects you can create with jQuery. You will learn how to fade and animate images and chain effects together.

Lesson One: Fading and Sliding

jQuery gives you the ability to **fade** images in and out. An element that is **fading** is gradually appearing or disappearing. There are several jQuery functions that cover fading in, fading out, toggling fading, and fading up to a certain point. You can also **slide** elements, which means the elements appear or disappear by shrinking or growing up or down.

The Fading Functions

Fading means an image is gradually appearing or disappearing without moving around. The jQuery functions **fadeIn()**, **fadeOut()**, **fadeToggle()**, and **fadeTo()** give you good control over fading.

fadeIn()	Makes an element gradually appear over 400 milliseconds. You can add a parameter "fast", "slow", or a number to change the timing.
fadeOut()	Makes an element gradually disappear over 400 milliseconds. You can add a parameter "fast", "slow", or a number to change the timing.
fadeToggle()	Will automatically make the element fade in if it's hidden or fade out if it's visible. Again the default timing is 400 milliseconds, but you can change that.
fadeTo()	This function always needs 2 parameters. The first is the duration ("fast", "slow", or a number). The second is a number between 0.0 and 1.0. 1.0 means the image is fully solid and 0.0 means the image is fully hidden (see-through). So **fadeTo("slow",0.2)** will slowly make the image fade until it is 20% visible.

The images below from left to right show an element that is faded to 20% (0.2), 50% (0.5), and 80% (0.8).

  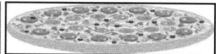

The fading function work much like **show()**, **hide()**, and **toggle()**, so we can update our pizza and breadsticks example to show fading instead.

```javascript
// attach a JavaScript function to the click event on the add button
$("#addBreadsticksButton").click(function()
{
    // make the breadsticks fade in solid quickly
    $("#breadsticks").fadeTo("fast",1.0);
    $("#addBreadsticksButton").hide();
    $("#removeBreadsticksButton").show();
});
// attach a JavaScript function to the click event on the remove button
$("#removeBreadsticksButton").click(function()
{
    // make the breadsticks image fade to 10% slowly
    $("#breadsticks").fadeTo(1000,0.1);
    $("#addBreadsticksButton").show();
    $("#removeBreadsticksButton").hide();
});
```

When the "Remove" button is clicked the **fadeTo()** command will fade the breadsticks image to 10% (0.1) over 1 second.

Then when "Add" is clicked the **fadeTo()** function will quickly fade the image back to fully visible (100% or 1.0).

Once you use **fadeTo()** to reach a certain level of visibility like 50% (0.5), that level is the new "visible" setting for that element. So if you **show()** or **fadeIn()** afterwards, it will only reach that new level (50%). You can use **fadeTo()** to change the level back to fully visible (100% or 1.0).

Work with Me: Fading Funny Fish 2

Your "Funny Fish 2" page has one button called "Fade In/Out" that we haven't used yet. Now that you know about fading effects, let's finish that now.

1. Open "Scripts/funnyfish2.js" in Komodo Edit.

2. In your existing "$(document).ready()" function, add another **click**() event function for the "#fade" button.

```javascript
$("p").mouseout(function () {
    $("p").css("text-shadow","none");
});


$("#fade").click(function() {
    $("#funnyfish2_3").fadeToggle(1000);
});

});
```

3. Save your changes to "funnyfish2.js" and reload "funnyfish2.html" in your web browser. Does the "Fade in/out" button now work correctly? Clicking the button once should fade the fish to become invisible. Clicking the button again will fade it back in to a solid image.

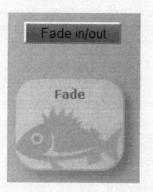

You can experiment with "fast" and "slow" or other numeric values for the **fadeToggle**() method to see how they change the behavior.

The Sliding Functions

Sliding an element is another way of hiding or showing it on the page. Instead of fading in or out, the element appears to shrink to nothing when hiding or grow to full size when becoming visible.

slideDown()	Makes an element appear by sliding down over 400 milliseconds. You can add a parameter "fast", "slow", or a number to change the timing.
slideUp()	Makes an element disappear by sliding up over 400 milliseconds. You can add a parameter "fast", "slow", or a number to change the timing.
slideToggle()	Will automatically make the element slide down if it's hidden or slide up if it's visible. Again the default timing is 400 milliseconds, but you can change that.

The easiest way to remember "up" from "down" is to picture a set of blinds on a window in your house. You raise (slide up) the blinds to hide them, and lower (slide down) the blinds to make them visible again.

The slide functions will actually adjust the **height** property of the target element towards 0 (slideUp) or towards the initial height (slideDown). That can make some interesting – an unexpected – effects.

What happens if our breadsticks are hidden and we call **slideDown()** on the image element directly? The image height will begin at 0 and slowly increase. This means the image will start small and grow to full size.

```
$("#breadsticks").slideDown("slow");
```

This does not exactly look like a "slide down" effect, but it's what you see when you increase the height of the image.

To get a true "slide down" effect, we can wrap the image in another block element like a **<div>** and then use the slide effect on that **parent** element instead. The image height will be unchanged, but the parent height will grow from 0 to full size, exposing more of the internal image along the way.

```
<div style="border:2px solid black;" id="breadsticksWrapper">
    <img id="breadsticks" src="breadsticks.png"/>
</div>
```

Now that we've wrapped our image in a **<div>**, we can target that **<div>** with the **slideDown()** function.

```
$("#breadsticksWrapper").slideDown("slow");
```

Now this is what we want to see from a function named **slideDown()**!

The **slideUp()** and **slideToggle()** functions work the same way, adjusting the height of the target element between 0 and full size. You can get different effects by targeting the element itself or a parent element.

Work with Me: Fading and Sliding Otter

At the end of the last chapter you created an "Otters" page with an image and a "Start" and "Stop" button. The button **click()** functions hide and show the image right now, but you can make some improvements using the jQuery fading and sliding functions.

4. Open "Scripts/otter.js" in Komodo Edit and find the existing function for the "#start" button.
5. Replace the existing call to **hide()** with a call to **fadeOut()** as shown below.

```
$("#start").click(function() {
    $("#otterImg").hide(2000);
    $("#otterImg").fadeOut("slow");
});
```

6. Next, find the function for the "#stop" button and replace the existing call to **show**() with a **fadeIn**().

```
$("#stop").click(function() {
    $("#otterImg").show(1000);
    $("#otterImg").fadeIn("fast");
});
```

7. Save your changes to "otter.js" and reload "otter.html" in your web browser. Click on the "Start" button to see the image fade out. Then click on "Stop" to bring it back.

8. Now in "otter.js", change the "#stop" function again to use **fadeTo**() instead of **fadeIn**().

```
$("#stop").click(function() {
    $("#otterImg").fadeIn("fast");
    $("#otterImg").fadeTo(1000,0.5);
});
```

9. Save your changes and reload "otter.html" again. Click on "Start" to hide the image, and then "Stop" to show it again. The image should come back half-way (50% or 0.5).

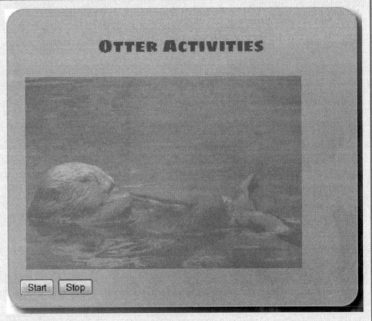

10. You can play with other parameters for **fadeIn()**, **fadeOut()**, and **fadeTo()** to make sure you understand how each function works.

11. Next we want to use **slideUp()** and **slideDown()**. In "otter.js", change your "#start" function to use **slideUp()** and your "#stop" function to use **slideDown()** as shown below.

```
$("#start").click(function() {
    $("#otterImg").fadeOut("slow");
    $("#otterDiv").slideUp("slow");
});
$("#stop").click(function() {
    $("#otterImg").fadeTo(1000,0.3);
    $("#otterDiv").slideDown("fast");
});
```

Notice we are now selecting the parent "#otterDiv" instead of the "#otterImage" directly.

12. Save your changes and reload "otter.html" to test out these new functions. Clicking "Start" should hide the image by sliding upwards, and clicking "Stop" should bring it back down again.

You can again experiment with different values for the speed of **slideUp()** and **slideDown()**. You can also try replacing one of the buttons with a **slideToggle()** and the other with a **fadeToggle()**. That way you can see both the slide and the toggle effects just by clicking on one button or the other.

Lesson Two: Timing and Multiple Effects

Chaining is the ability to link two or more functions into a single action, within a single statement. When you do this, the browser only has to find the element once through the selector. Then it calls each function in turn on that element. To chain methods together, you use a period as a joiner. In this example we find the "breadsticksWrapper" element and then call both **slideUp()** and **slideDown()** functions on it.

```
$("#breadsticksWrapper").slideUp(500).slideDown(500);
```

These lines can get quite long, so you can add a carriage return (new line) after each function call to make everything easier to read and understand.

```
$("#breadsticksWrapper")
    .slideUp(500)
    .slideDown(500)
    .fadeOut(500)
    .fadeIn(500);
```

Notice that you only place a semicolon once on the last line to mark the end of the statement. All of these lines combine to form a single JavaScript statement, so you only use one semicolon.

The Delay Function

When chaining functions together, you might want to add a pause or delay in between effects. The jQuery **delay()** function will do just that! The parameter to the **delay()** function is the number of milliseconds you want to pause. The example below will pause for 1 second (1000 milliseconds) after the **slideUp()** is finished before **slideDown()** begins.

```
$("#breadsticksWrapper").slideUp(5000).delay(1000).slideDown(5000);
```

The **delay()** function will only work when placed between functions using some sort of timed effect. For example, calling **hide()** or **show()** with no parameters will complete instantly, and adding a delay between them will have no effect.

```
$("#breadsticksWrapper").hide().delay(1000).show();     // NO EFFECT
```

The Stop Method

Let's say you have started a long animation sequence. You might want to allow the user to stop the animation before it finishes. To do this you can provide another button such as "Stop" and then call the jQuery **stop()** function on the element that is animating.

```
$("#startBreadsticks").click(function()
{
    $("#breadsticksWrapper")
        .slideUp(5000)
        .delay(1000)
        .slideDown(5000)
        .delay(1000)
        .fadeIn(3000)
        .delay(2000)
        .fadeOut(3000);
});

$("#stopBreadsticks").click(function()
{
    $("#breadsticksWrapper").stop();
});
```

At this point you might be wondering why we're going to so much trouble with a breadsticks image. Well, we just really like yummy breadsticks! Now, in the example above, our "breadsticksWrapper" element is going to start a long series of function calls with several slides, delays, and fades when the user clicks on a "startBreadsticks" button. If the user clicks on the "stopBreadsticks" button, what will happen?

The **stop()** function by itself will halt the currently running animation only. So if you happened to be in the middle of a **fadeIn()**, that animation would stop immediately, and the browser would continue to the next effect. If you want **stop()** to halt all animations that are waiting to begin, add a **true** parameter like this:

```
$("#breadsticksWrapper").stop(true);
```

Now as soon as that **stop()** function is called, all animations that are ready to run on the selected element will be removed completely. Keep in mind that halting an animation sequence in the middle might leave your web page in a weird state. It's hard to predict when the user will choose to stop things, and your elements might not be useable or easy to see afterwards.

Work with Me: Finishing the Otter

Your "Otters" page has only demonstrated one effect at a time. But now with chaining, we can put together several functions that run when the "Start" button is clicked. We can also use the "Stop" button to halt the animation in the middle.

1. Open your existing "Scripts/otter.js" file in Komodo Edit.
2. Find your existing **click()** function for the "#start" button. It currently has just one effect on the "#otterDiv" element. Remove that one effect, and add the chained function calls shown below starting with the **fadeTo()** command.

```
$("#start").click(function() {
    $("#otterDiv").slideToggle("slow");
        .fadeTo("slow",0.4)
        .delay(1000)
        .fadeTo("fast",1)
        .hide(1000)
        .delay(1000)
        .show(1000)
        .delay("slow")
        .slideUp(4000)
        .delay("slow")
        .slideDown(500);
});
```

3. Next, find the **click()** function for your "#stop" button. Replace the one effect you have there with a call to **stop(true)** to halt all animation.

```
$("#stop").click(function() {
    $("#otterDiv").slideDown("fast");
    $("#otterDiv").stop(true);
});
```

4. Save your changes to "otter.js" and reload "otters.html" in your browser. Test the "Start" and "Stop" buttons; do they work as expected? When clicking "Start" you should see the image fade out slowly to 40% (0.4), then fade back in quickly to fully visible. Next the image is hidden, then shown, and then hidden and shown again with sliding. At the end the image should be back to normal size and visibility.

It's hard to capture an animation sequence as a series of pictures. The two images to the right show a couple of steps you might see during your full chain of effects.

When you click "Stop" the animation should halt immediately and not continue with any other effects, because we put the **true** parameter in the parentheses to **stop()**. If you need to restore the image to start over, you can reload the HTML page in your browser.

Lesson Three: jQuery Animation

The fading and sliding functions give you some creative ways to show and hide an element. If you want to create other interesting effects you can use the jQuery **animate()** function to control other CSS properties.

The jQuery animate() Function

The **animate()** function works mostly on numeric CSS properties such as **width**, **height**, or **font-size**. The values for these properties are numbers like *100px*, *50px*, or *16px*. You cannot **animate()** properties that have text values like **float**: *left* or **color**: *blue*. You also cannot animate shorthand properties like **border** that combine several properties into one string such as *2px solid blue*.

What does **animate()** actually do? It changes a numeric CSS property from the current value to a new value over a period of time. So you could change the **width** and **height** to make an element grow or shrink, or change the **top** and **left** positions to make it move around the screen. The syntax for **animate()** is a little unusual, so let's review it carefully.

```
$(selector).animate({properties},duration);
```

The *selector* is your standard CSS selector to choose your target element; nothing unusual there. The *duration* at the end is also your standard "fast" or "slow" or number in milliseconds like 2000 for 2 seconds. The *properties* you want to animate are placed in a list in between opening and closing curly braces { and }.

A list of properties can have one or more name-value pairs, where the name is the CSS property name, and the value is the new numeric value for the property such as "10px" or "100%". Each name is separated from the value with a colon ":" and the value is in single or double quotes. Commas separate name-value pairs. The examples below show one and two properties in a list.

> {property1: "value1"}
> {property1: "value1", property2: "value2"}

The example below changes the breadsticks image element **width** to *0px* over 2 seconds.

```
$("#breadsticks").animate({width: "0px"},2000);
```

Let's get a bit more creative and make the breadsticks image "fly" off the screen towards the top-left corner when the "Remove" button is clicked. We can use the **css**() function to change the **position** to *absolute* and then **animate**() the **top** and **left** values to large negative numbers over 2 seconds.

```
$("#removeBreadsticksButton").click(function()
{
    // make the breadsticks image fly away
    $("#breadsticks").css("position","absolute");
    $("#breadsticks").animate({top: "-999px", left: "-999px"},2000);
    $("#addBreadsticksButton").show();
    $("#removeBreadsticksButton").hide();
});
```

Since the -999px, -999px position is far to the top and left of the screen, clicking the "Remove" button will cause the breadsticks image to fly off in that direction over 2 seconds.

Camel Case

Your **animate()** properties list contains names and values. Short CSS property names like **width**, **height**, **top**, and **left** match exactly with the **animate()** property names. However, if the CSS property name has a dash in it like **font-size** or **border-width**, then you cannot use that name exactly in JavaScript. You need to use "Camel Case" instead.

Camel Case means you get rid of the dash and capitalize the first letter of the second and remaining words.

- **font-size** becomes **fontSize**
- **border-width** becomes **borderWidth**
- **border-top-width** becomes **borderTopWidth**
- **margin-left** becomes **marginLeft**

The new names seem to have humps like a camel, so that's why it's called Camel Case.

Using Whitespace

If you want to **animate()** many properties at once it can be hard to read a very long statement on a single line. So you can use some carriage returns (new lines) to make it easier to read. Notice both examples below are still a single statement with one semi-colon at the end.

```
$("#breadsticks").animate({top: "-999px", left: "-999px"},2000);
$("#breadsticks").animate({
    top: "-999px",
    left: "-999px"
    },2000);
```

Both statements do the same thing. You can pick a style that works best for you.

Relative Values

When you **animate()**, your values can contain **absolute** numbers like "-999px" or "100%". That means **animate()** will start from the current value and end up at the absolute value. You can also use **relative** values like "-=100px" or "+=50px". A relative value will make an addition or subtraction to the current value. So "+=50px" means add 50 pixels to the current value and "-=100px" means subtract 100px from the current value.

When using relative values,

- "-=" (minus-equals) at the beginning means subtract from the current value
- "+=" (plus-equals) at the beginning means add to the current value

In this example, we move the breadsticks image up and to the left by subtracting 100 pixels from the current **top** and **left** positions.

```
$("#breadsticks").animate({top: "-=100px", left: "-=100px"},2000);
```

We can change the example so the second value adds 50px to the current **width**.

```
$("#breadsticks").animate({top: "-=100px", width: "+=50px"},2000);
```

As a result the image will move straight up (-100 pixels) and get 50 pixels wider.

Work with Me: Octopus Animation

You are going to practice your **animate**() skills on a new "Octopus" page. You can copy the files from the Activity Starters directory first, and then get to work on the JavaScript functions.

1. Using Windows Explorer or Mac OS Finder, copy the following files from your "Activity Starters/Chapter13" directory:

   - "octopus-animation.html" to "MyProjects/Aquamaniacs"
   - "SiteStyle/octopus-animation.css" to "MyProjects/Aquamaniacs/SiteStyle"
   - "SiteStyle/octopus-animation.png" to "MyProjects/Aquamaniacs/SiteStyle"
   - "SiteStyle/grid.gif" to "MyProjects/Aquamaniacs/SiteStyle"
   - "Scripts/octopus-animation.js" to "MyProjects/Aquamaniacs/Scripts"

1. Load "octopus-animation.html" into your web browser to see the page layout.

The "MainContent" area contains a **<div>** with a grid as a background image. Inside that **<div>** is another **<div>** with an octopus image. Two buttons at the bottom will allow the users to start two different animation sequences. You will complete the first sequence now, and come up with another on your own at the end of the chapter.

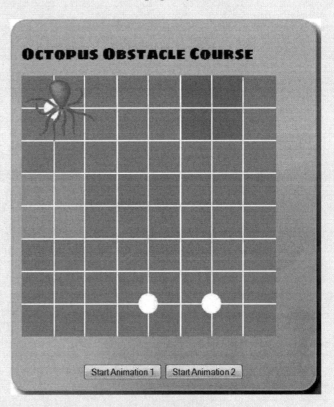

2. If you look at "octopus-animation.html" in Komodo Edit, you will see the "MainContent" HTML is fairly short. The grid image comes from CSS rules applied to the "grid" **<div>**. The octopus image comes from the CSS applied to the "octopus" **<div>**, so your **animate**() functions will want to select the "octopus" element also.

```html
<div id="MainContent">

    <h1>Octopus Obstacle Course</h1>

    <div id="grid">
        <div id="octopus"></div>
    </div>


    <p> </p>
    <div id="button">
        <button id="animate1">Start Animation 1</button>
        <button id="animate2">Start Animation 2</button>
    </div>

</div><!-- end of MainContent -->
```

3. Open the "Scripts/octopus-animation.js" file in Komodo Edit. We have already created the "$(document).ready()" function and a **click**() function for each button. Right now all of your code will go on the "animate1" **click**() function.

```javascript
// run this function when the first animation button is clicked
$("#animate1").click(function() {

    // your code here...

});
```

4. Let's start with a simple, single-step animation. Add the following line inside the **click**() function to move the octopus to the right.

```javascript
// your code here...
$("#octopus").animate({left:'225px'},1000);
```

5. Save your JavaScript changes and reload "octopus-animation.html" in your web browser. Your octopus should move to the right when you click on "Start Animation 1".

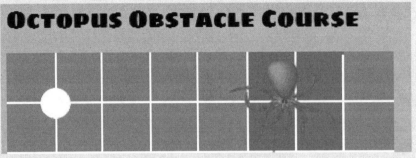

6. Next, add three more **animate**() commands underneath the first one.

```
$("#octopus").animate({left:'225px'},1000);
$("#octopus").animate({top:'295px'},2000);
$("#octopus").animate({left:'120px'},1000);
$("#octopus").animate({top:'55px',},2000);
```

7. Save your changes and reload your HTML page. When you click "Start", the octopus should now move to the right, down to the bottom, left a little bit, and then back up towards the middle.

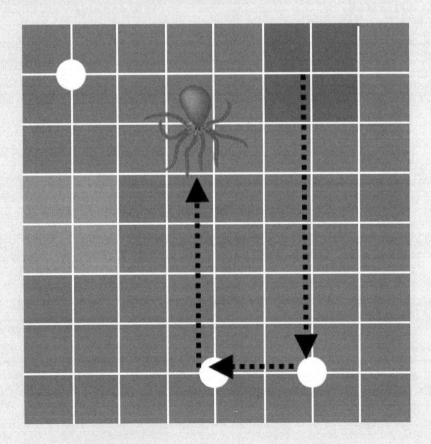

8. Next, add a final animation step right below your last statement.

```
$("#octopus").animate({top:'55px',},2000);
$("#octopus").animate({
    height:'300px',
    width:'300px',
    opacity:'0.0'
    },4000);
```

This time we are animating three different properties. We are growing the **width** and **height** to 300px each, and also changing the **opacity** to 0.0. The opacity is a measure of how transparent or see-through an image appears, so this change will make the octopus seem to fade away.

9. Save your changes and check out the results!

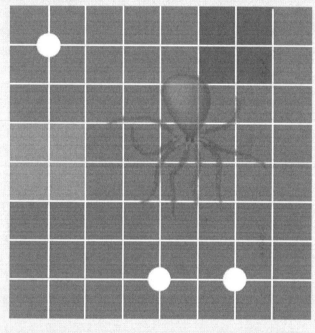

10. You'll notice that once the animation is complete, you don't see anything else by clicking on the button. That's because the octopus is still large and invisible. You can add one more **animate()** statement to the very beginning of your function to reset the octopus to the initial values.

```
// your code here...
$("#octopus").animate({
    top: '0px',
    left: '0px',
    width: '100px',
    height: '86px',
    opacity:'1.0'
    },0);
```

Now you can click on the "Start Animation 1" button many times, and each time it will reset the octopus image to the beginning before starting the rest of the animation.

Chapter Review

- jQuery **fading** functions allow you to gradually show or hide an element.
- jQuery **sliding** functions allow you to show or hide an element by changing the height.
- The **fadeToggle()** and **slideToggle()** functions will automatically change an element from hidden to visible and back again.
- **Chaining** means you can call multiple jQuery functions on elements from a one selector statement.
- You can use the **delay()** function to add a pause between jQuery effects.
- The jQuery **stop()** function will halt the currently running effect or all effects on an element.
- The jQuery animate() function can adjust numeric values over time for many CSS properties.
- Each **animate()** call will take a list of name-value pairs to animate over a certain duration.
- Use Camel Case naming for CSS property names in JavaScript
- You can **animate()** with absolute values that end at the target number.
- You can **animate()** with relative values to add or subtract the given number from the current value.

Your Turn Activity: Dancing Octopus

In this activity you are going to add a second animation of your own design to the Octopus page.

Your activity requirements and instructions are found in the "Chapter_13_Activity.pdf" document located in your "KidCoder/AdvancedWebDesign/Activity Docs" folder. You can access this document through your Student Menu or by double-clicking on it from Windows Explorer or Mac OS Finder.

Complete this activity now and ensure you understand the material before continuing!

Chapter Fourteen: Final Project

You now have a wide variety of important HTML5, CSS3, and JavaScript skills. It's time to put those to use on your own project! You have already completed one final project at the end of the first-semester course, so you have a good idea what to do.

For your final project, you can pick one of these things to do:

- **Extend your final project from the first semester**
- **Create a brand new website on a different topic**
- **Extend the Aquamaniacs website**

The topic for your final project website is up to you. We aren't going to give you a series of guided steps, because you have enough experience to figure out how to approach the design, layout, content, styling, and behavior on your own. Store your new project in a new folder under your "MyProjects" directory.

Your final project should at least:

- **Include three new web pages with a dynamic navigation menu between them**
- **Demonstrate several new HTML5 elements, including <nav> and <footer>**
- **Use several new CSS3 styles and selectors**
- **Show multi-media (video and/or sounds) on at least one page**
- **Include JavaScript and jQuery behavior on at least one page**

You can find or make the images and other content on your own. You are welcome to use any of the images, sounds, or videos from the Aquamaniacs project in your own final project. You can also look in your "Activity Starters/Chapter14" directory to find some aquatic images that we didn't use in the Aquamaniacs website.

Don't forget it's easier to modify an existing project instead of creating something brand new from scratch. So you may want to start with a copy of your "Aquamaniacs" project and modify those files as needed.

This should be fun, so pick a topic you enjoy and show off your skills!

What's Next?

Congratulations, you have finished *KidCoder™: Advanced Web Design*! This course completes our KidCoder: Web Design series. You now have the tools and experience you need to create your own simple websites using HTML5, CSS3, and JavaScript. You are encouraged to continue learning and exploring on your own.

We offer other KidCoder courses that teach Windows and Game programming using the Visual Basic language. Older students can begin our TeenCoder™ series that covers Windows, Game, and Android programming using the C# and Java languages.

We hope you have enjoyed this course produced by Homeschool Programming, Inc. We welcome student and teacher feedback at our website. You can also visit our website to request courses on other topics.

http://www.HomeschoolProgramming.com

Index